31-10
18.00

D1546655

CONCRETE COUNTRY RESIDENCES

Photographs and Floor Plans of Turn-of-the-Century Homes

CONCRETE COUNTRY RESIDENCES

Photographs and Floor Plans of Turn-of-the-Century Homes

ATLAS PORTLAND CEMENT COMPANY

DOVER PUBLICATIONS, INC.
Mineola, New York

Bibliographical Note

This Dover edition, first published in 2003, is an unabridged republication of the third edition of the work originally published by The Atlas Portland Cement Company, New York, in 1908 under the title *Concrete Country Residences* [first publication: 1906].

Library of Congress Cataloging-in-Publication Data

Concrete country residences : photographs and floor plans of turn-of-the-century homes / Atlas Portland Cement Company.—Dover ed.
    p. cm.
  Originally published: 3rd ed. New York : Atlas Portland Cement Co., 1908.
  ISBN 0-486-42733-1 (pbk.)
    1. Concrete houses—United States—Designs and plans. I. Atlas Portland Cement Company.

NA7205 .C66 2003
728.8'0973'09041—dc21

                                          2002072877

Manufactured in the United States of America
Dover Publications, Inc., 31 East 2nd Street, Mineola, N.Y. 11501

Concrete Country Residences

THE making of a home is an epoch in a career; and before that eventful time comes it is a good thing to make a careful investigation into the relative merits of building materials and to choose those which insure permanency as well as comfort and architectural beauty and strength.

Durability of material has at all times distinguished one nation above another, and it will be so for all time. Care and thought are well spent, therefore, in determining of what the walls of one's house shall be constructed, and the observing builder has come to acknowledge the superiority of CONCRETE from the view points of *economy* and *comfort*.

The economical advantage is always to be considered, and in this case it is certainly obvious on account of its remarkable durability, freedom from decay and the saving in the use of paint. The original cost will, of course, vary according to the location of the property, but it will be found that concrete in many forms can be built as cheap or cheaper than perishable wood. Should a house be looked upon as an investment, or with that individual affection with which a man regards his own home, a concrete building will be found to outclass all others, since it retains its original value for centuries, while other forms of construction rapidly depreciate.

Significant emphasis has been placed on the fireproof qualities of concrete construction, by the fact that in the great conflagrations of Baltimore and San Francisco, the concrete structures remained practically unharmed when the unquenchable walls of flame swept over and destroyed all other forms of buildings; and it is safe to predict that a large proportion of the city which shall rise out of the ashes of imperial San Francisco will be made of concrete.

In some States the cost of insurance of concrete buildings is extremely low, and in many instances owners have ceased to insure:—the dangers from storm, flood and fire being lessened in a proportionate degree.

Comfort, which has become one of the chief requirements of American living, has been found most in evidence in a concrete house, because the walls are rendered *warmer in winter, cooler in summer* and more completely sanitary than those built with any other material; and the adaptability of concrete to any form of architecture has been demonstrated to the satisfaction of builders everywhere.

The so-called "Mission Architecture," low-roofed, picturesque and suggestive of lower California in the romantic Spanish period, is familiar to all, and to many people the words "concrete residence" convey the idea of this style of architecture only; but the ease with which concrete can be moulded to any form, and the various modes of construction, including the solid wall, the hollow wall, the concrete blocks and stucco give this material a distinct advantage over other materials and make possible any style of architecture.

Solid wall construction is used in factories, warehouses and structures of like character, also in large country houses.

The hollow wall construction, which has been the occasion of lively interest to those studying modern building methods, consists of tying two comparatively thin walls together with concrete piers at regular intervals. This style, while slightly more expensive, is considered by many authorities the best form of construction for house-building purposes.

The great popularity of concrete has led to its adoption for building purposes in many parts of the country, and, since the Arts and Crafts have joined hands, and the plan of a house is made to conform to the general scheme of the landscape, the adaptability of this material to securing harmonious effects has been demonstrated—the combination of the three essentials which Vitruvius, the ancient authority on architecture, lays down as the qualities indispensable for a fine building—stability, utility, beauty.

It is an old saying that "cheap labor builds an expensive house," and while it is true that the unskilled workman under an experienced foreman may build a satisfactory structure, the designing and erection of concrete buildings should be undertaken, preferably, by architects who have made a special study of the material and its possibilities, in order to obtain the best results at the lowest cost.

Hollow concrete blocks are favored by many builders in various localities; and if made by competent and reliable people, that style of concrete is satisfactory. Stucco, a lighter, less expensive form of concrete construction, is also extensively used at the present time, commonly applied over rough stone, brick, wood or metal lath.

ATLAS Portland Cement is considered by the leading architects and engineers as the Standard American Brand. It is *always uniform*, invariably reliable and satisfactory, and easy to work. An examination of the beautiful effects obtained, together with the confidence placed in the quality by users of this brand of cement, explains its popularity and accounts for the output of over 14,000,000 barrels of **ATLAS** Portland Cement for 1908, which is greater than the combined output of any other four cement companies in the world.

The growing interest of home makers in concrete houses has led us to publish this book as a guide to those who are about to build, with the hope that the illustrations and descriptions contained in its pages will assist them in successfully planning their future residences of concrete, thus assuring themselves that their homes will be proof against the destroying elements of frost, flood and flame, and will combine the qualities of comfort, permanency and beauty.

THE **ATLAS** PORTLAND CEMENT COMPANY.

HOTEL BLENHEIM, ATLANTIC CITY, N. J.   Price & McLanahan, Architects
Solid Reinforced Concrete

Residence of Murray Guggenheim, West End, New Jersey

Stucco on Metal Lath

Carrere & Hastings, Architects

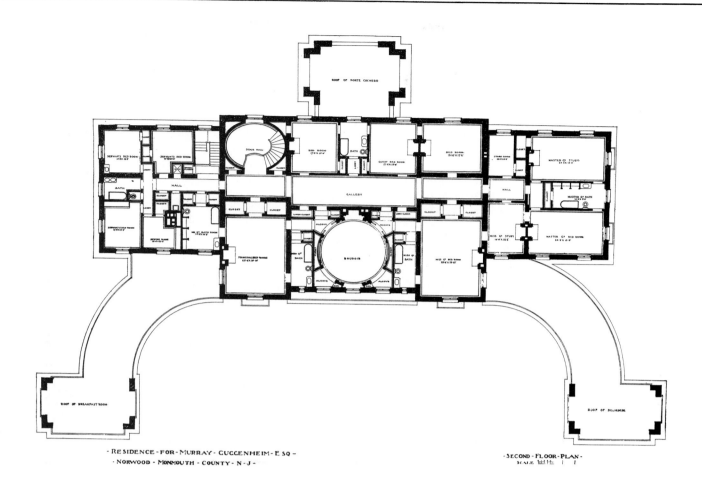

- RESIDENCE · FOR · MURRAY · GUGGENHEIM · ESQ -
- NORWOOD · MONMOUTH · COUNTY · N · J -

- SECOND · FLOOR · PLAN -
SCALE

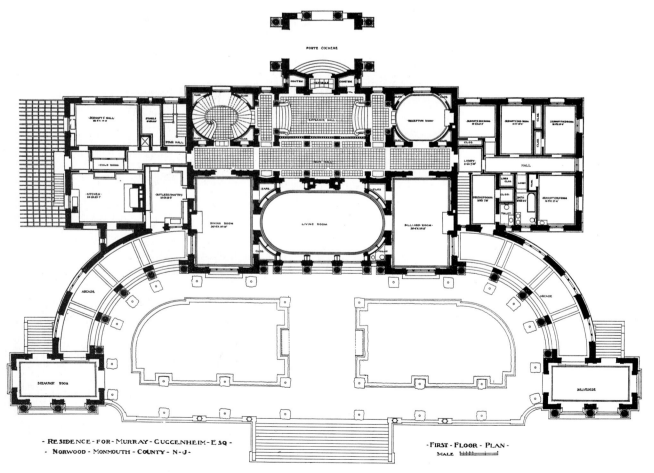

- RESIDENCE · FOR · MURRAY · GUGGENHEIM · ESQ -
- NORWOOD · MONMOUTH · COUNTY · N · J -

- FIRST · FLOOR · PLAN -
SCALE

11

RESIDENCE OF S. SACHS, ELBERON, N. J.

Stucco on Metal Lath

J. H. Freedlander, Architect

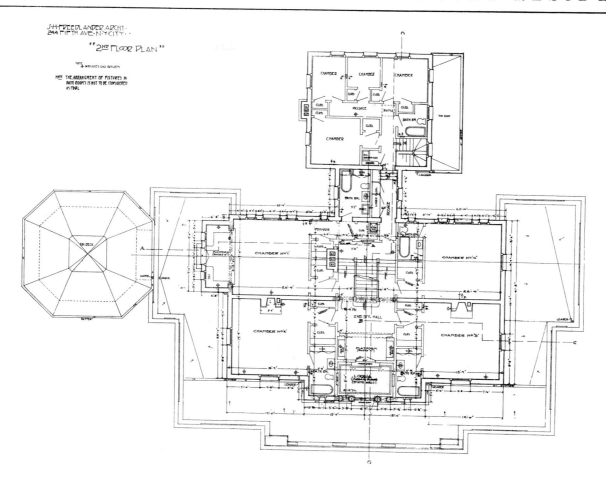

J·H·FREEDLANDER·ARCHT·
244·FIFTH·AVE·N·Y·CITY··

"2ND FLOOR PLAN"

NOTE
◆ INDICATES GAS OUTLETS

NOTE: THE ARRANGEMENT OF FIXTURES IN
BATH ROOMS IS NOT TO BE CONSIDERED
AS FINAL

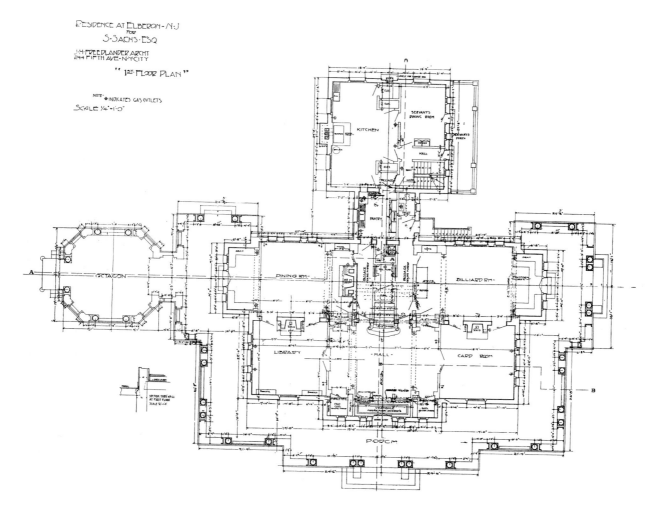

RESIDENCE AT ELBERON·N·J
FOR
S·SACHS·ESQ

J·H·FREEDLANDER·ARCHT
244·FIFTH·AVE·N·Y·CITY

"1ST FLOOR PLAN"

NOTE: ◆ INDICATES GAS OUTLETS
SCALE ¼"=1'-0"

RESIDENCE OF H. M. FLAGLER, PALM BEACH, FLA.　　Stucco on Metal Lath　　Carrere & Hastings, Architects

14

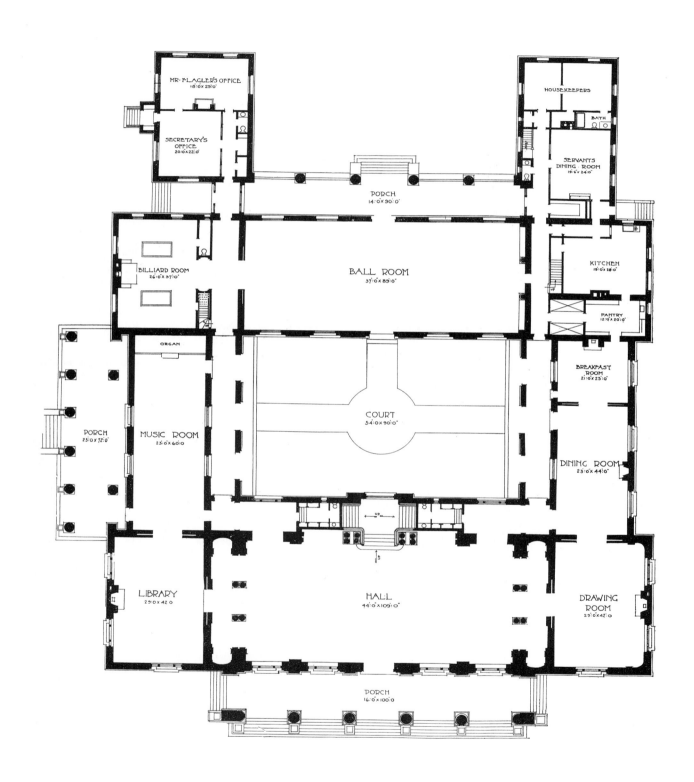

MR· FLAGLER'S OFFICE
18'·0" X 25'·0"

SECRETARY'S
OFFICE
20'·0" X 22'·0"

HOUSEKEEPERS

BATH

SERVANTS
DINING · ROOM
19'·6" X 24'·0"

PORCH
14'·0" X 90'·0"

BILLIARD ROOM
26'·0" X 37'·0"

BALL ROOM
37'·0" X 85'·0"

KITCHEN
19'·0" X 26'·0"

PANTRY
12'·0" X 20'·0"

ORGAN

BREAKFAST
ROOM
21'·0" X 23'·0"

PORCH
23'·0" X 72'·0"

MUSIC ROOM
23'·0" X 60'·0"

COURT
54'·0" X 90'·0"

DINING ROOM
23'·0" X 44'·0"

UP

LIBRARY
23'·0" X 42'·0"

HALL
44'·0" X 109'·0"

DRAWING
ROOM
23'·0" X 42'·0"

PORCH
16'·0" X 100'·0"

RESIDENCE OF A. S. CARHART, TUXEDO PARK, N. Y.   Stucco on Metal Lath   Trowbridge & Livingston, Architects

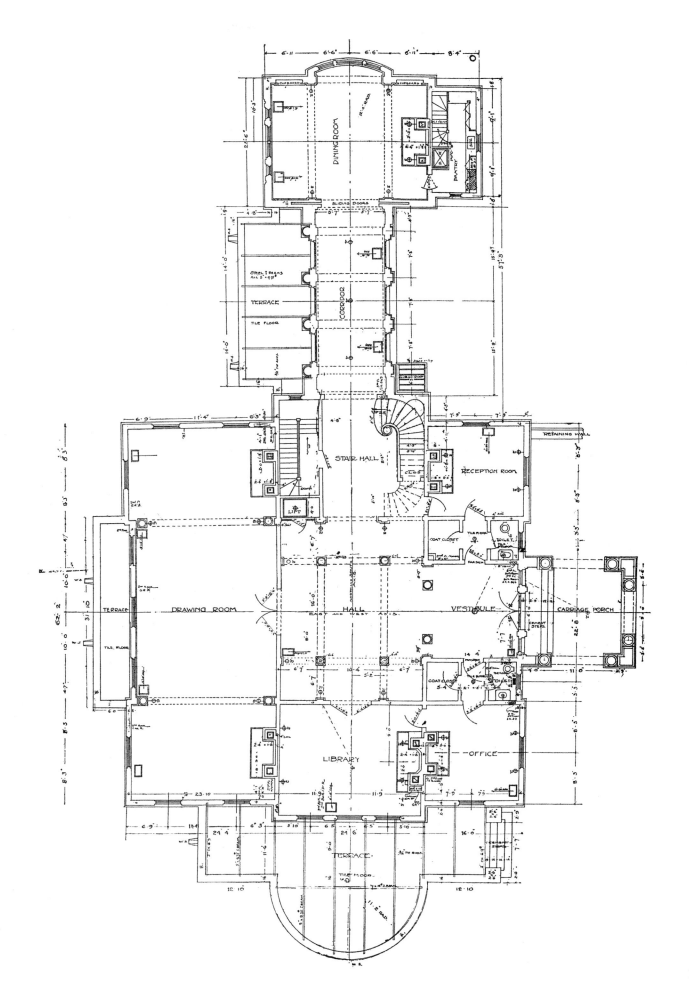

RESIDENCE OF N. F. PALMER, PORTCHESTER, N. Y.   Stucco on Metal Lath

F. H. Dodge, Architect
Pottier & Stymus Co., Consulting Architects

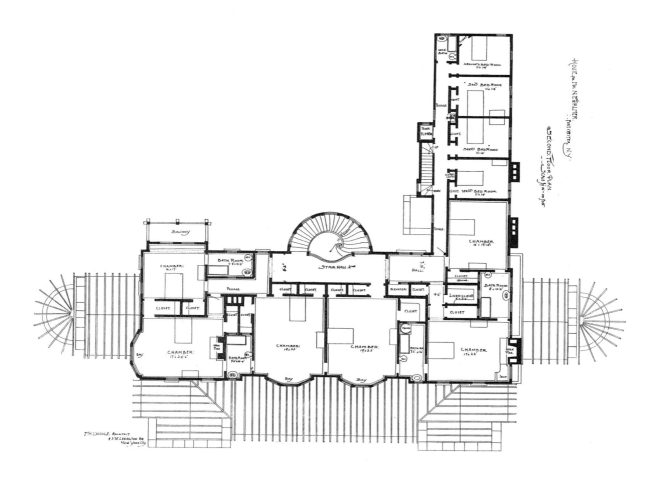

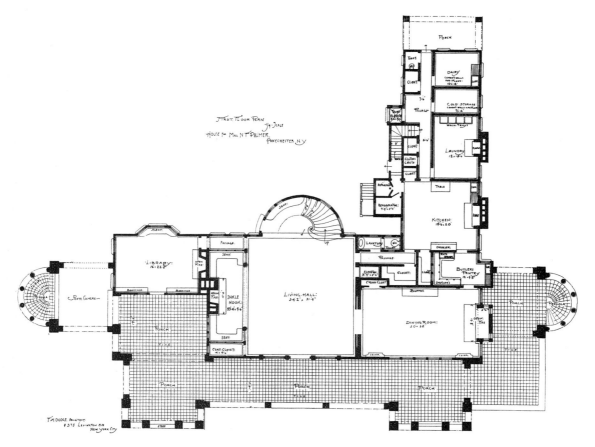

F. H. Dodge, Architect
Pottier & Stymus Co., Consulting Architects

Stucco on Metal Lath

Residence of Geo. Q. Palmer, Portchester, N. Y.

20

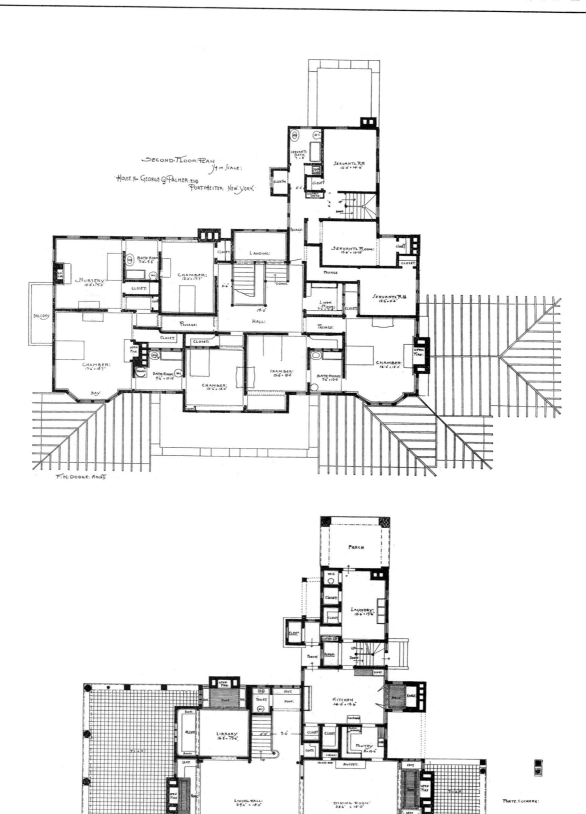

Second Floor Plan ¼ in. Scale.
House for George Q. Palmer, Esq.
Portchester, New York.

First Floor Plan ¼ in. Scale
House for George Q. Palmer, Esq. Portchester New York

Residence of F. F. Palmer, Portchester, N. Y.

Stucco on Metal Lath

F. H. Dodge, Architect
Pottier & Stymus Co., Consulting Architects

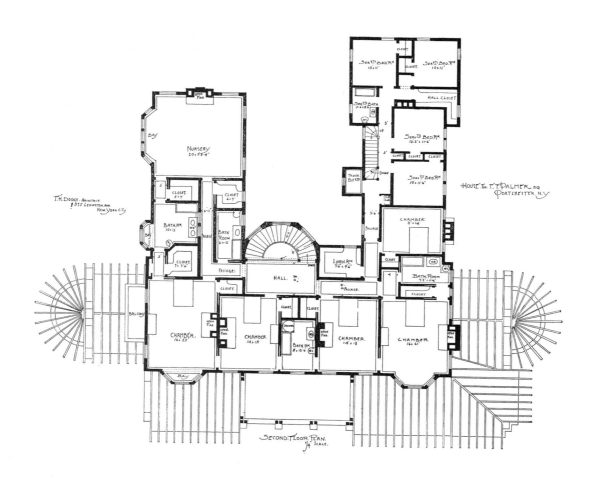

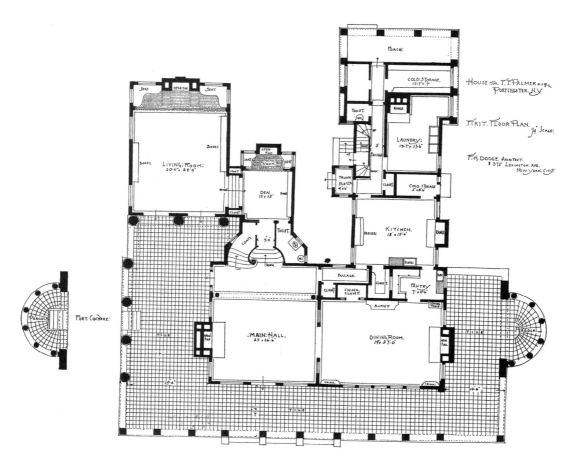

Residence of O. M. Mitchell, Montclair, N. J.   Stucco on Metal Lath   N. Le Brun & Sons, Architects

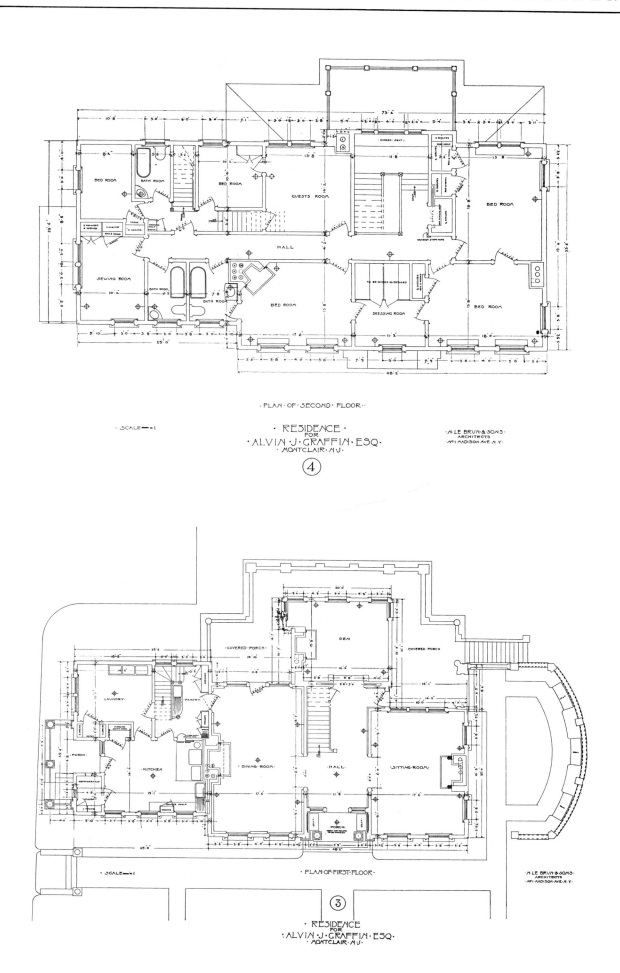

· PLAN · OF · SECOND · FLOOR ·

· SCALE ─ ─1

· RESIDENCE ·
FOR
· ALVIN · J · GRAFFIN · ESQ ·
MONTCLAIR · N·J·

·N·LE BRUN·& SONS·
ARCHITECTS
Nº 1 MADISON·AVE·N·Y·

④

· SCALE ─ ─1

·PLAN·OF·FIRST·FLOOR·

·N·LE BRUN·& SONS·
ARCHITECTS
Nº 1 MADISON·AVE·N·Y·

③

· RESIDENCE ·
FOR
·ALVIN·J·GRAFFIN·ESQ·
·MONTCLAIR·N·J·

RESIDENCE OF C. D. DU BOIS, MONTCLAIR, N. J.　　Stucco on Metal Lath　　N. Le Brun & Sons, Architects

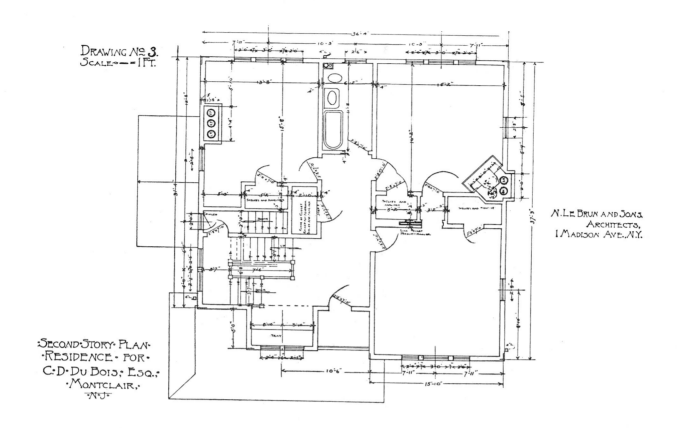

DRAWING № 3.
SCALE — 1 FT.

N. LE BRUN AND SONS,
ARCHITECTS,
1 MADISON AVE., N.Y.

·SECOND·STORY·PLAN·
·RESIDENCE·FOR·
·C·D·DU BOIS, ESQ.,
·MONTCLAIR,·
·N·J·

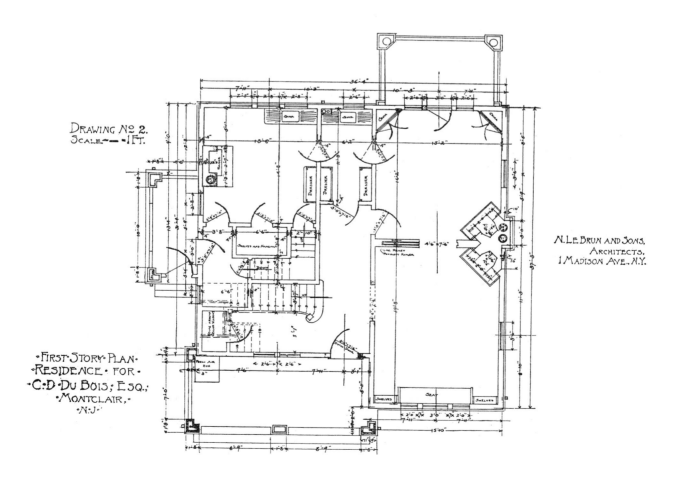

DRAWING № 2.
SCALE — 1 FT.

N. LE BRUN AND SONS,
ARCHITECTS,
1 MADISON AVE., N.Y.

·FIRST·STORY·PLAN·
·RESIDENCE·FOR·
·C·D·DU BOIS, ESQ.,
·MONTCLAIR,·
·N·J·

RESIDENCE OF EMMET QUEEN, GLEN COVE, L. I.   C. P. H. Gilbert, Architect
Stucco on Brick

STABLE AT THE RESIDENCE OF EMMET QUEEN, GLEN COVE, L. I. C. P. H. Gilbert, Architect
Stucco on Brick

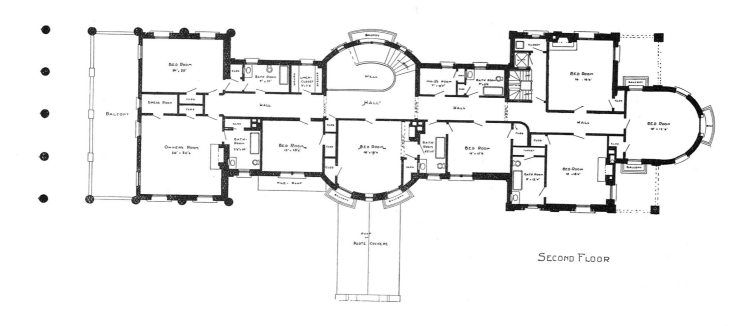

Second Floor

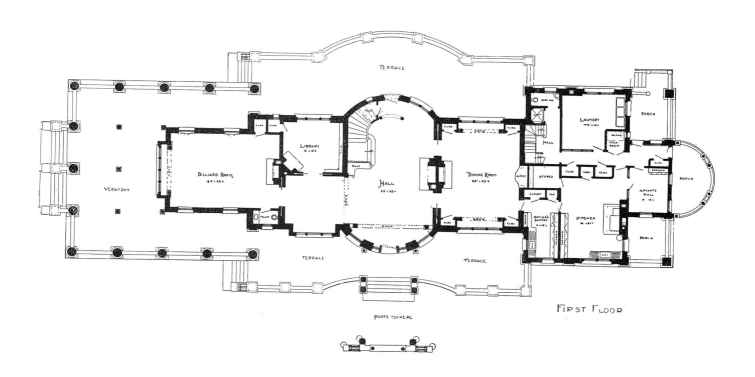

First Floor

RESIDENCE OF W. H. KNIGHT, BRISTOL, R. I.

Carl P. Johnson, Architect
Parkhurst & Kissam, Consulting Architects

Solid Reinforced Concrete

BOAT HOUSE OF W. H. KNIGHT, BRISTOL, R. I.

Carl P. Johnson, Architect
Parkhurst & Kissam, Consulting Architects

Solid Reinforced Concrete

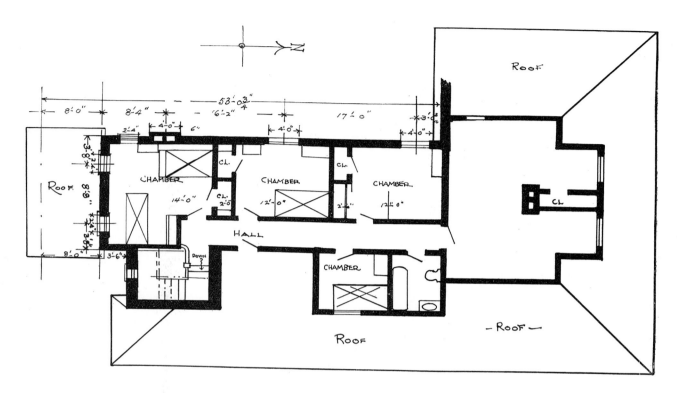

SECOND FLOOR PLAN

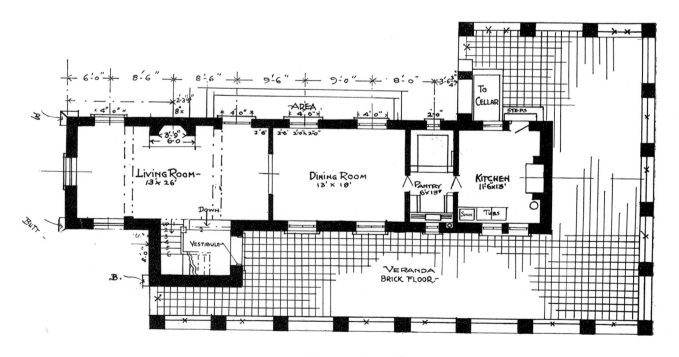

FIRST FLOOR PLAN

RESIDENCE OF ALBERT KAHN, DETROIT, MICH.   Albert Kahn, Architect
Solid Reinforced Concrete
Front View

Rear View

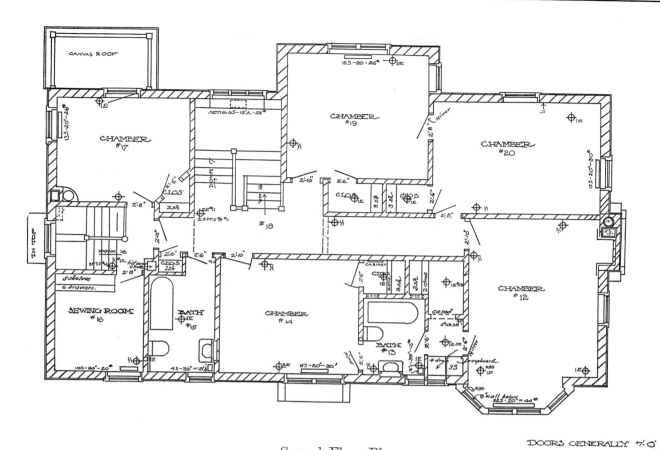

Second Floor Plan

DOORS GENERALLY 7'-0"

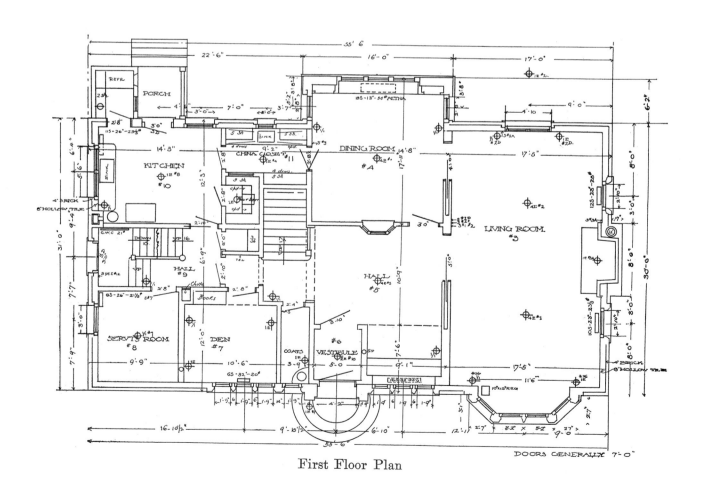

First Floor Plan

DOORS GENERALLY 7'-0"

RESIDENCE OF E. CHANDLER WALKER, WALKERVILLE, ONT.   Albert Kahn, Architect
Solid Reinforced Concrete

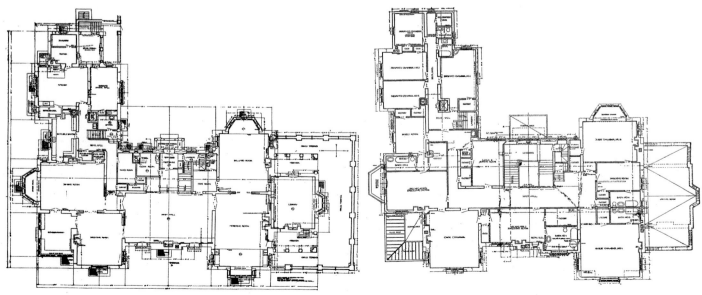

First Floor Plan   Second Floor Plan

RESIDENCE OF FRED PABST, OCONOMOWOC, WIS.
Solid Reinforced Concrete

Fernekes & Cramer, Architects

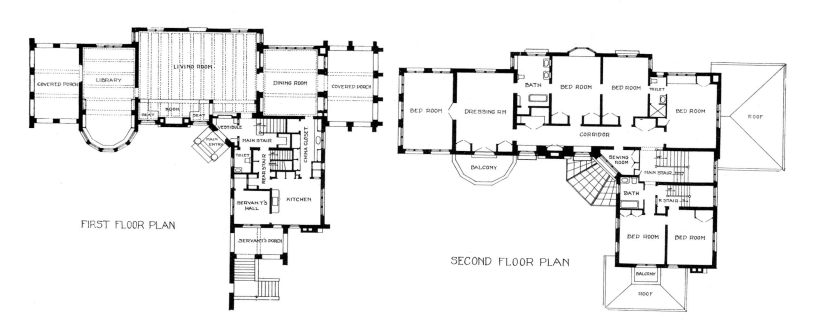

FIRST FLOOR PLAN

SECOND FLOOR PLAN

RESIDENCE OF D. L. YOUNGS, SUMMIT, N. J.
Stucco on Metal Lath

Wm. K. Benedict, Architect

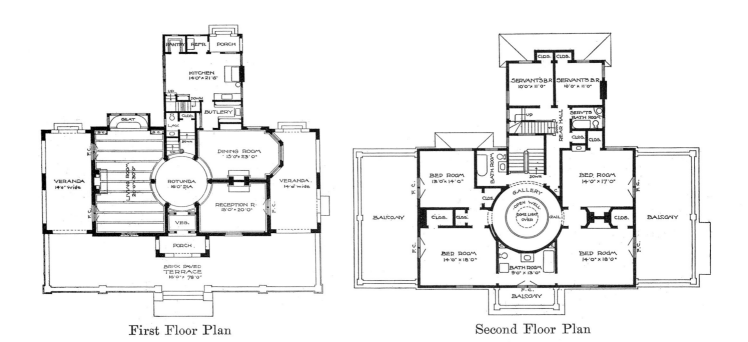

First Floor Plan

Second Floor Plan

RESIDENCE OF CHARLES E. CHURCHILL, MONTCLAIR, N. J.
Solid Reinforced Concrete

Christopher Myers, Architect

First Floor Plan

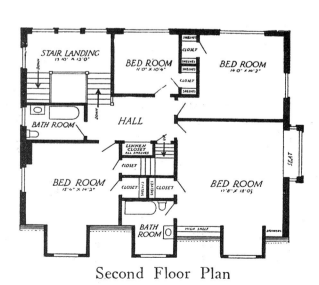

Second Floor Plan

RESIDENCE OF THE LATE J. A. BAILEY, MOUNT VERNON, N. Y.   VanVleck & Goldsmith, Architects
Stucco on Brick

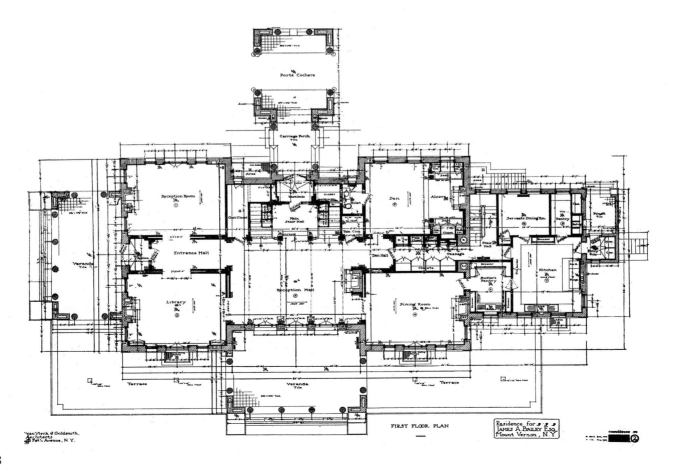

FIRST FLOOR PLAN

RESIDENCES OF MR. TOWNSEND AND MR. COLE, BALTIMORE, MD.
Stucco on Metal Lath

Ellicott & Emmart, Architects

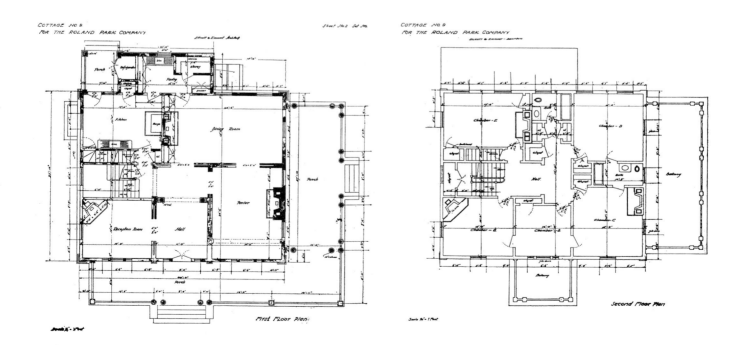

RESIDENCE OF F. P. HOLRAN, ENGLEWOOD, N. J.
Stucco on Metal Lath

Wm. K. Benedict, Architect

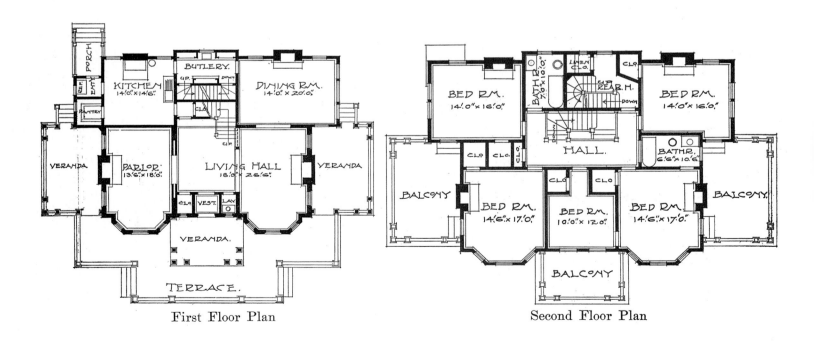

First Floor Plan

Second Floor Plan

RESIDENCE OF GEO. HOADLEY, JR., CINCINNATI, OHIO
Stucco on Metal Lath

Elzner & Anderson, Architects

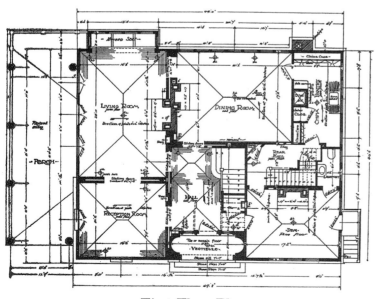

First Floor Plan

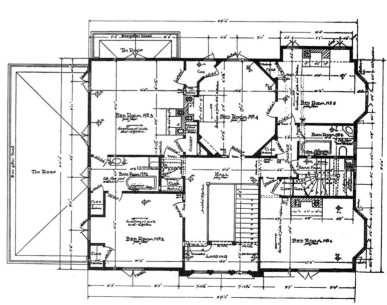

Second Floor Plan

RESIDENCE OF D. R. CRAIG, WELLESLEY, MASS.   W. D. Brown, Architect
Stucco on Metal Lath

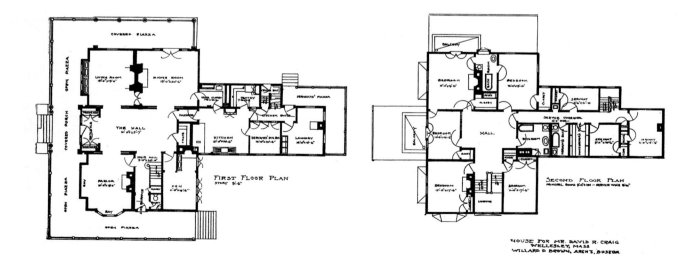

FIRST FLOOR PLAN

SECOND FLOOR PLAN

HOUSE FOR MR. DAVID R. CRAIG
WELLESLEY, MASS
WILLARD D BROWN, ARCH'T, BOSTON.

RESIDENCE OF F. B. LOVEJOY, MONTCLAIR, N. J.
Stucco on Metal Lath

A. F. Norris, Architect

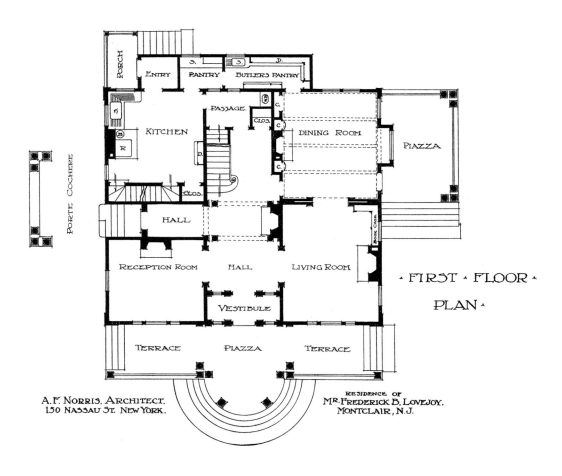

· FIRST · FLOOR ·

PLAN ·

A.F. NORRIS, ARCHITECT.
150 NASSAU ST. NEW YORK.

RESIDENCE OF
MR. FREDERICK B. LOVEJOY.
MONTCLAIR, N.J.

RESIDENCE OF R. H. CLARKE, MOBILE, ALA. G. B. Rogers, Architect
Stucco on Metal Lath

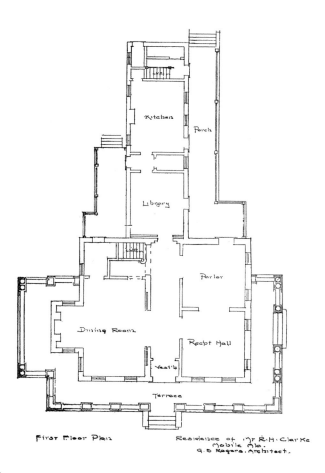

First Floor Plan Residence of Mr R. H. Clarke
Mobile Ala.
G. B. Rogers, Architect.

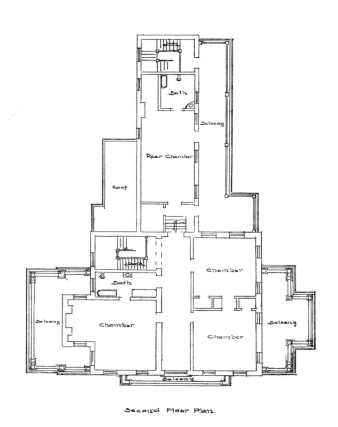

Second Floor Plan.

Residence of Mr R. H. Clarke
Mobile Ala.
G. B. Rogers, Architect.

CHAPEL AT AURIESVILLE, AURIESVILLE, N. Y.
Solid Reinforced Concrete

Ballinger & Perrot, Architects

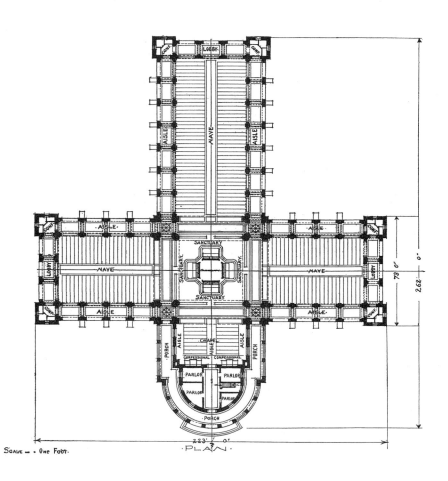

SCALE — ONE FOOT.
·PLAN·

RESIDENCE OF A. L. JOHNSON, FT. HAMILTON, N. Y.   Little & O'Connor, Architects
Stucco on Metal Lath

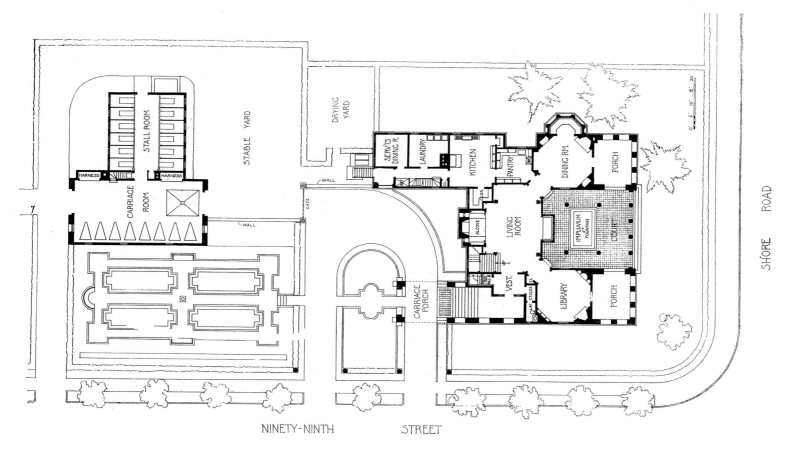

RESIDENCE OF CLINTON MACKENZIE, OYSTER BAY, L. I.
Stucco on Brick

Clinton Mackenzie, Architect

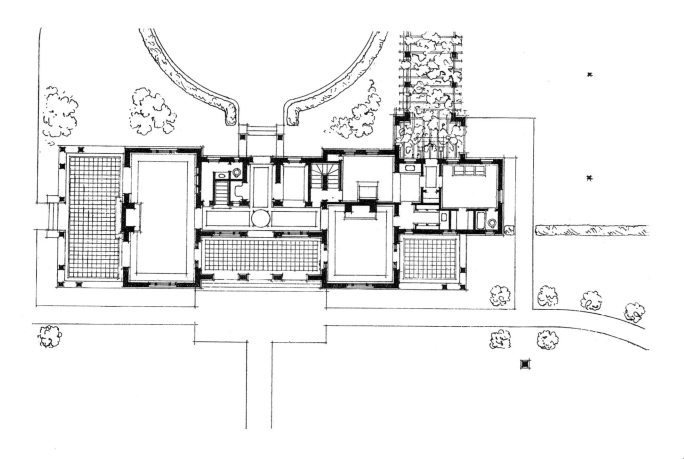

RESIDENCE OF ALFRED MITCHELL, JAMAICA, W. I. I.
Solid Reinforced Concrete

Chapman & Frazer, Architects

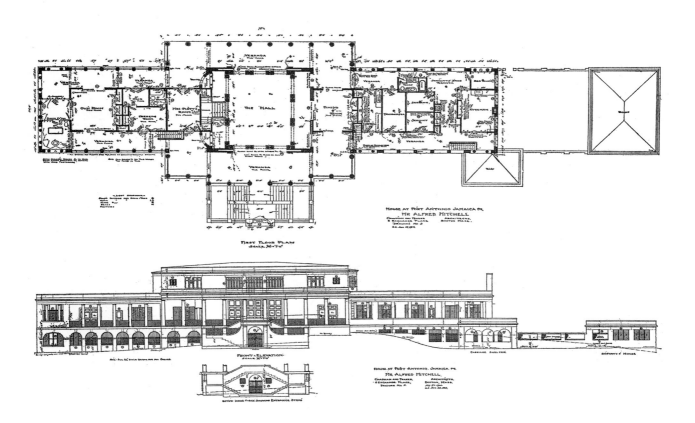

ITALIAN VILLA, MONTCLAIR, N. J.

Stucco on Metal Lath

A. F. Norris, Architect

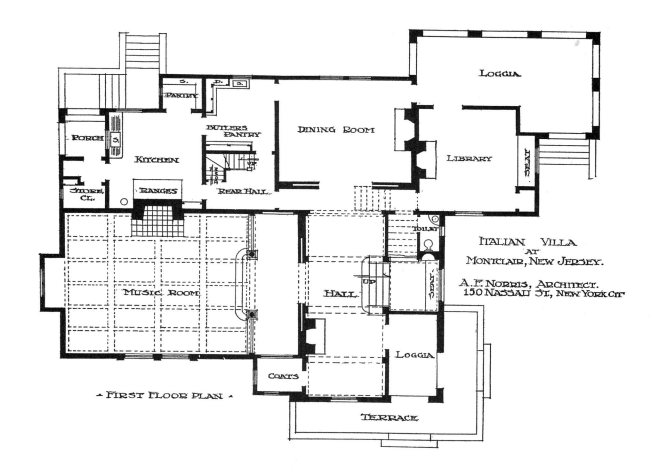

ITALIAN VILLA
AT
MONTCLAIR, NEW JERSEY.
A. F. NORRIS, ARCHITECT.
150 NASSAU ST, NEW YORK CITY

FIRST FLOOR PLAN

RESIDENCE ON ROCKLEDGE ROAD, MONTCLAIR, N. J.   A. F. Norris, Architect
Stucco on Metal Lath

- FIRST FLOOR PLAN -

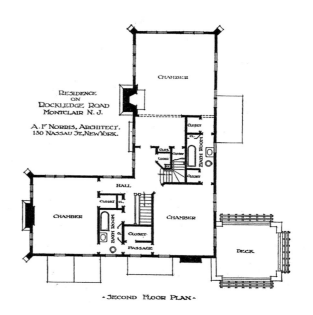

- SECOND FLOOR PLAN -

Constructed by the L. B. Valk Archt. Co., Los Angeles, Cal.
Rubble Concrete and Stucco on Metal Lath

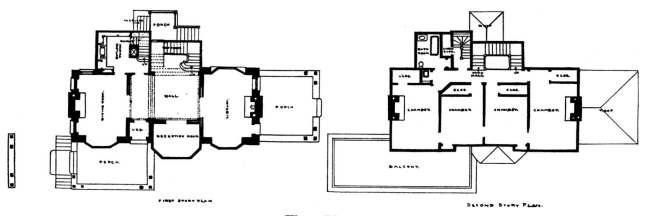

Floor Plans

RESIDENCE OF C. L. EATON, CLIFTON, MASS.   Chapman & Frazer, Architects
Stucco on Metal Lath

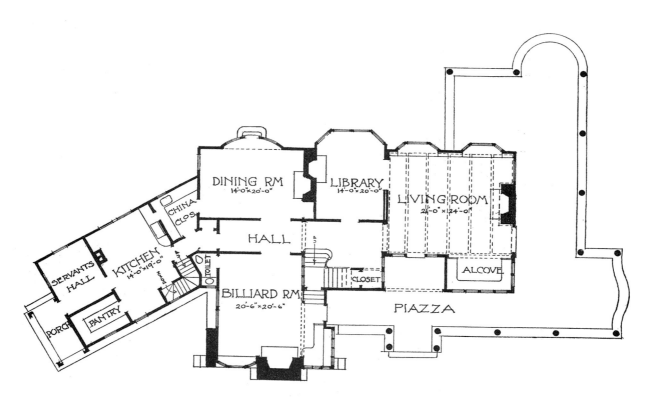

FIRST FLOOR PLAN

HOUSE AT CLIFTON MASS
CHAPMAN & FRAZER ARCHTS BOSTON

RESIDENCE OF D. D. WALKER, KENNEBUNKPORT, ME.   Chapman & Frazer, Architects
Stucco on Metal Lath

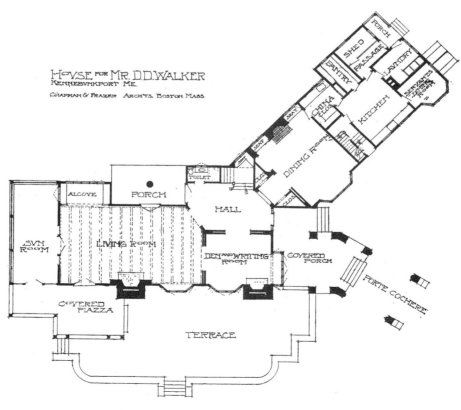

PLAN OF FIRST FLOOR

RESIDENCE OF C. S. HOUGHTON, CHESTNUT HILL, MASS.
Stucco on Metal Lath

Chapman & Frazer, Architects

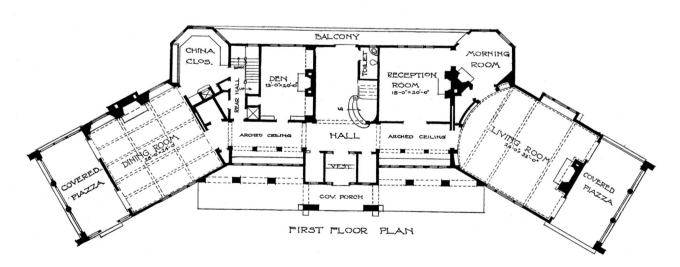

FIRST FLOOR PLAN

HOUSE AT CHESTNUT HILL MASS
CHAPMAN & FRAZER ARCHTS BOSTON

RESIDENCE OF E. N. FOSS, COHASSET, MASS.   Chapman & Frazer, Architects
Stucco on Metal Lath

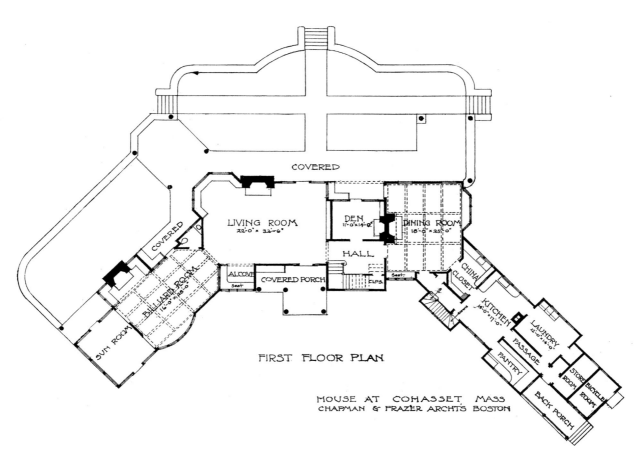

FIRST FLOOR PLAN

HOUSE AT COHASSET MASS
CHAPMAN & FRAZER ARCHT'S BOSTON

Residence of F. C. Hood, Brookline, Mass.
Stucco on Metal Lath

Chapman & Frazer, Architects

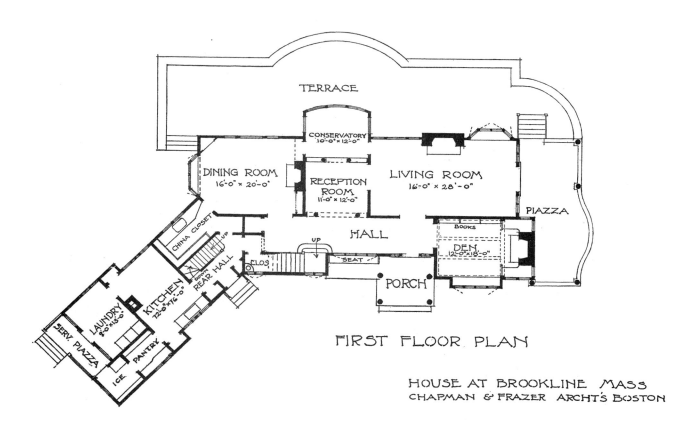

FIRST FLOOR PLAN

HOUSE AT BROOKLINE MASS
CHAPMAN & FRAZER ARCHT'S BOSTON

RESIDENCE OF WM. FLETCHER, BROOKLINE, MASS.   Chapman & Frazer, Architects
Stucco on Metal Lath

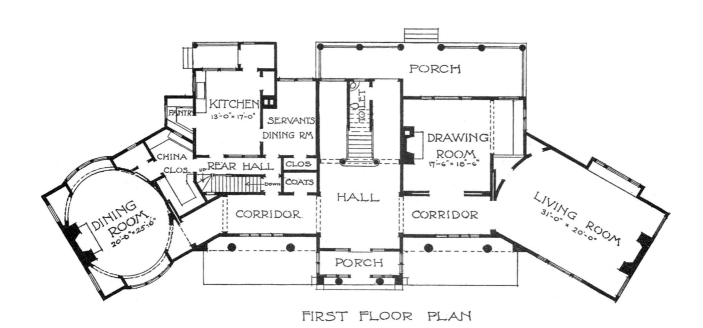

FIRST FLOOR PLAN

HOUSE AT BROOKLINE MASS
CHAPMAN & FRAZER ARCH'TS BOSTON

RESIDENCE OF J. R. STEERS, GREENWICH, CONN.
Solid Concrete Block Construction

Blake & Butler, Architects

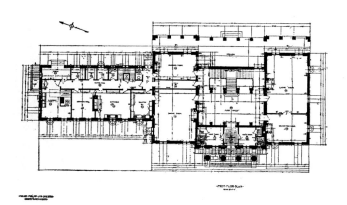

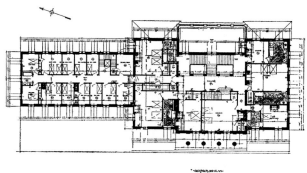

RESIDENCE OF A. S. YORK, NEW HAVEN, CONN.   Brown & Von Beren, Architects
Solid Concrete Block Construction

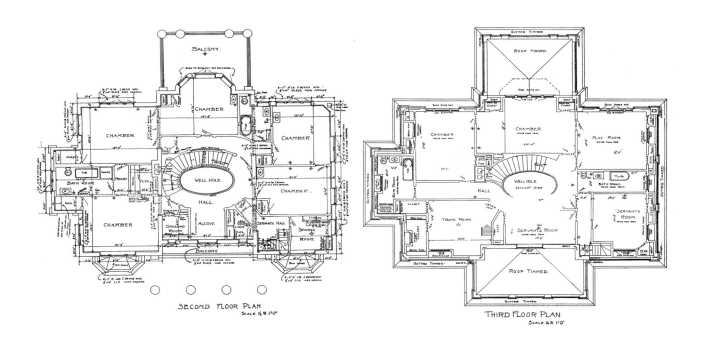

SECOND FLOOR PLAN
Scale ⅛ = 1'0"

THIRD FLOOR PLAN
Scale ⅛ = 1'0"

RESIDENCE OF C. T. IVES, MONTCLAIR, N. J.
Stucco on Metal Lath

A. F. Norris, Architect

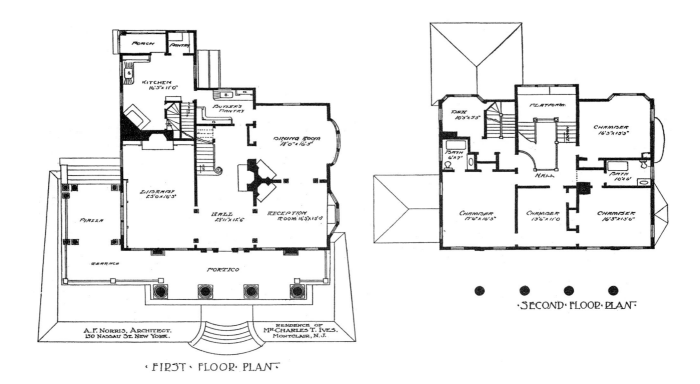

· FIRST · FLOOR · PLAN ·

· SECOND · FLOOR · PLAN ·

RESIDENCE OF A. T. STILSON, MONTCLAIR, N. J.   A. F. Norris, Architect
Stucco on Metal Lath

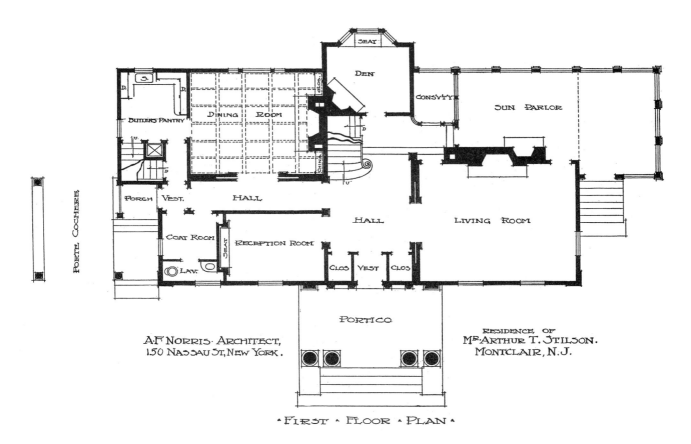

A. F. NORRIS· ARCHITECT,
150 NASSAU ST, NEW YORK.

RESIDENCE OF
MR. ARTHUR T. STILSON.
MONTCLAIR, N. J.

·FIRST·FLOOR·PLAN·

RESIDENCE OF E. Y. BLISS, BOSTON, MASS.   Clough & Wardner, Architects
Stucco on Metal Lath

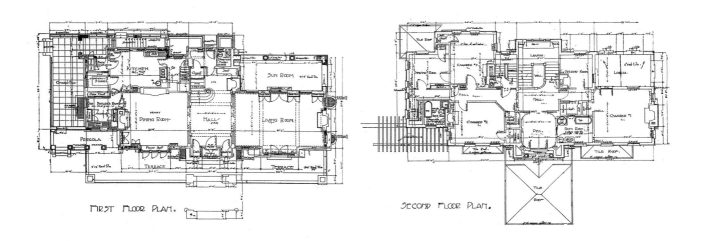

FIRST FLOOR PLAN.   SECOND FLOOR PLAN.

RESIDENCE OF EDWARD BURNETT, PETERBORO, N. H.   Edward Burnett, Architect
Stucco on Metal Lath

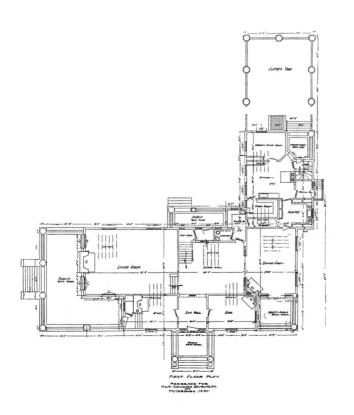

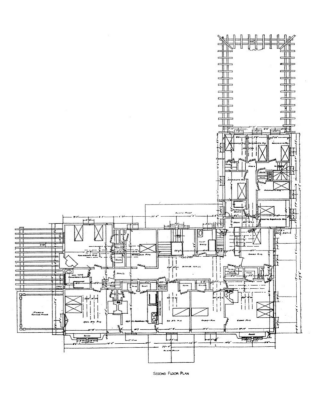

RESIDENCE OF R. M. DYAR, GROSSE POINTE, MICH.
Stucco on Metal Lath

A. W. Chittenden, Architect

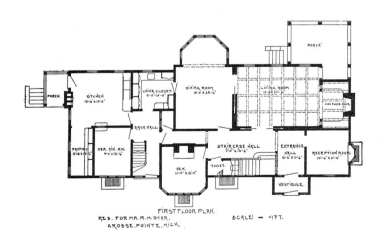

RESIDENCE OF H. K. WHITE, MILTON, MASS.   Chapman & Frazer, Architects
Stucco on Metal Lath

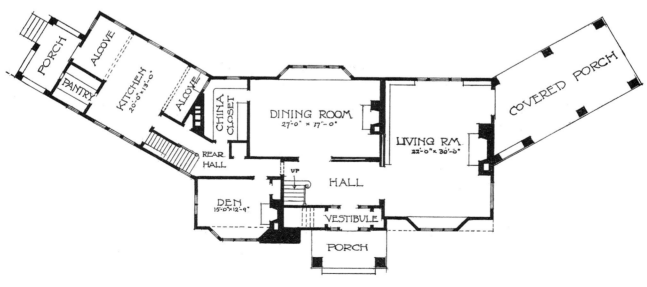

FIRST FLOOR PLAN

HOUSE AT MILTON MASS
CHAPMAN & FRAZER ARCH'TS BOSTON

RESIDENCE OF J. E. WING, MECHANICSBURG, OHIO   E. E. Holman, Architect
Solid Reinforced Concrete

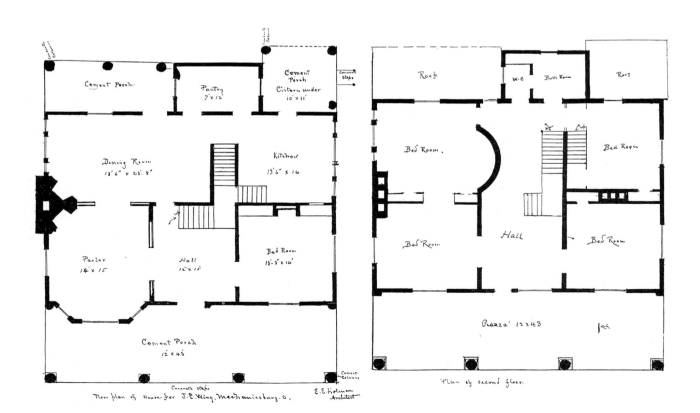

RESIDENCE OF J. F. ADAMS, WHEELING, W. VA.
Stucco on Metal Lath

Ed. B. Franzheim, Architect

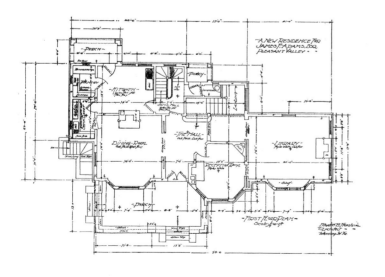

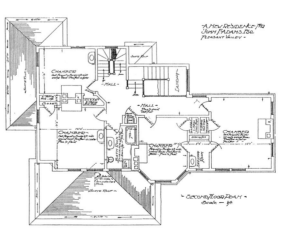

RESIDENCE OF C. K. PARMLEE, KENILWORTH, ILL.
Geo. W. Maher, Architect
Stucco on Metal Lath

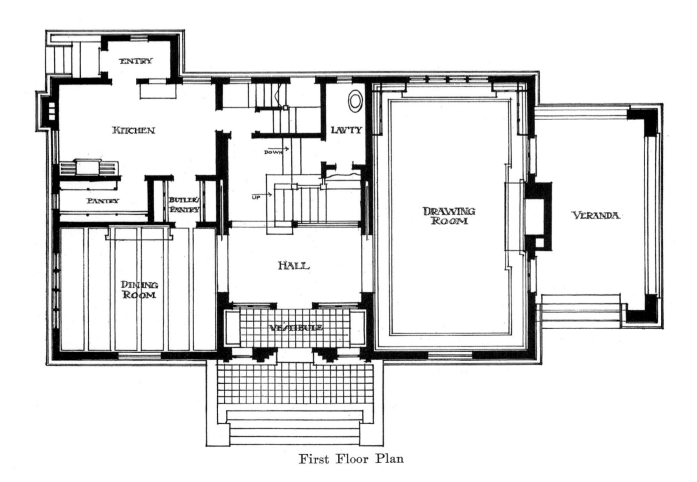

First Floor Plan

RESIDENCE OF F. N. CORBIN, KENILWORTH, ILL.   Geo. W. Maher, Architect
Stucco on Metal Lath

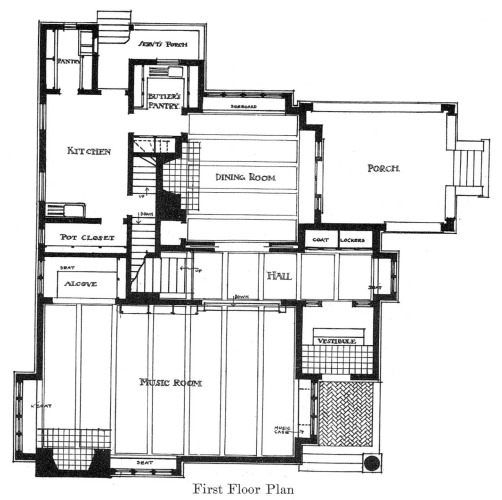

First Floor Plan

RESIDENCE OF CHAS. W. SCHICK, BUENA PARK, ILL.   Jenney, Mundie & Jensen, Architects
Solid Reinforced Concrete

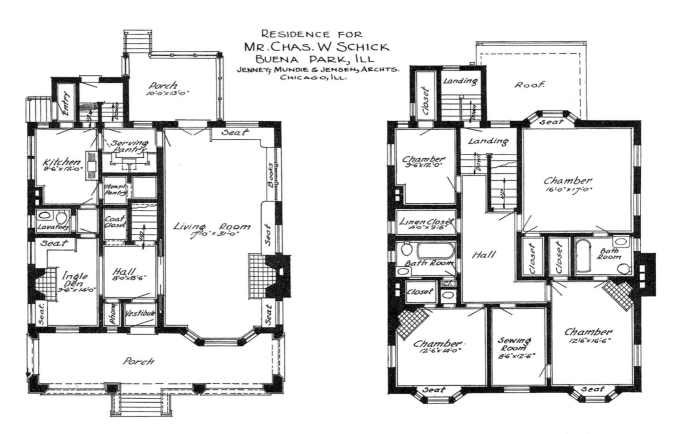

First Floor Plan   *Second Floor Plan*

RESIDENCE OF C. R. BOWMAN, TOLEDO, OHIO

H. W. Wachter, Architect

Stucco on Metal Lath

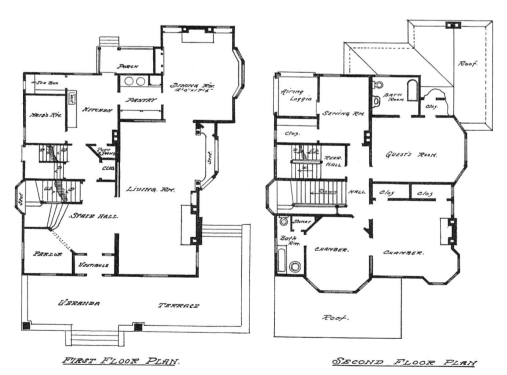

FIRST FLOOR PLAN.

SECOND FLOOR PLAN

RESIDENCE
of
MR CHAS. R. BOWMAN.
TOLEDO, OHIO.
Harry W. Wachter — Arch't.
71 The Nasby Toledo, O.

RESIDENCE OF N. R. CLARK, MOBILE, ALA.   Stone Bros., Architects
Stucco on Metal Lath

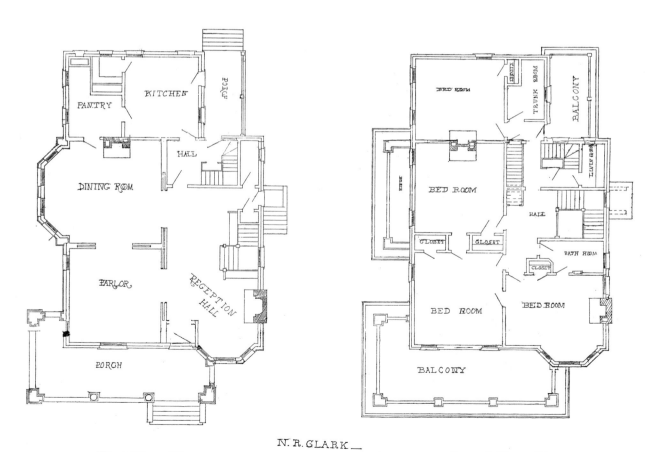

First Floor Plan   N. R. CLARK   Second Floor Plan

RESIDENCE OF C. L. LAURETTA, MOBILE, ALA.   Geo. B. Rogers, Architect
Stucco on Metal Lath

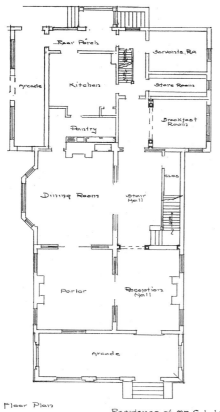

First Floor Plan   Residence of Mr C. L. Lauretta
Mobile Ala.
G. B. Rogers Architect.

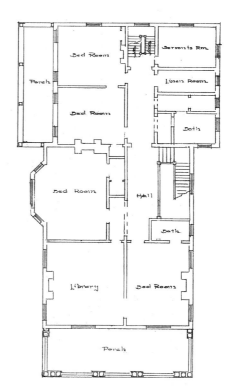

Second Floor Plan   Residence of Mr C. L. Lauretta
Mobile Ala.
G. B. Rogers Architect

RESIDENCE OF J. E. DAMEREL, MONTCLAIR, N. J.   A. F. Norris, Architect
Stucco on Metal Lath

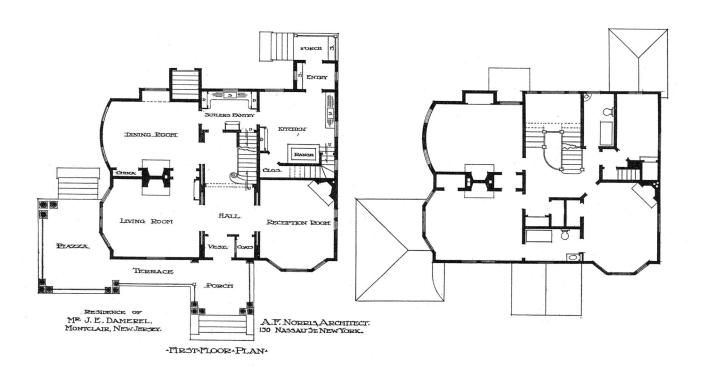

RESIDENCE OF
MR. J. E. DAMEREL,
MONTCLAIR, NEW JERSEY.

A. F. NORRIS, ARCHITECT.
150 NASSAU ST. NEW YORK.

·FIRST·FLOOR·PLAN·

RESIDENCE OF MRS. BACHRACH, WASHINGTON, D. C.
Stucco on Metal Lath

Wood, Donn & Deming, Architects

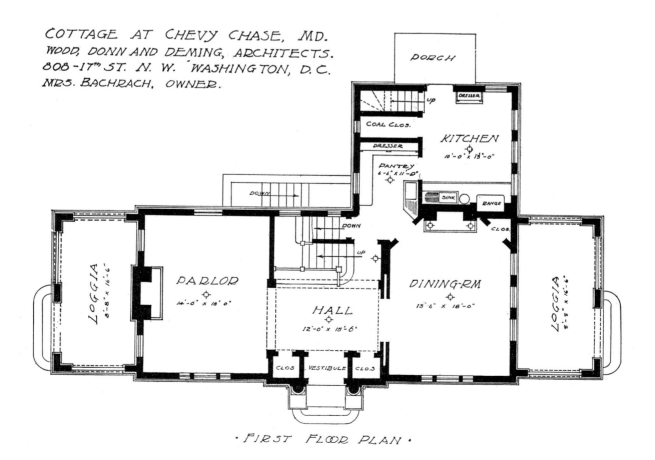

COTTAGE AT CHEVY CHASE, MD.
WOOD, DONN AND DEMING, ARCHITECTS.
808-17ᵗʰ ST. N. W. WASHINGTON, D. C.
MRS. BACHRACH, OWNER.

· FIRST FLOOR PLAN ·

RESIDENCE OF M. CHENEY, KENILWORTH, ILL.   Geo. W. Maher, Architect
Stucco on Metal Lath

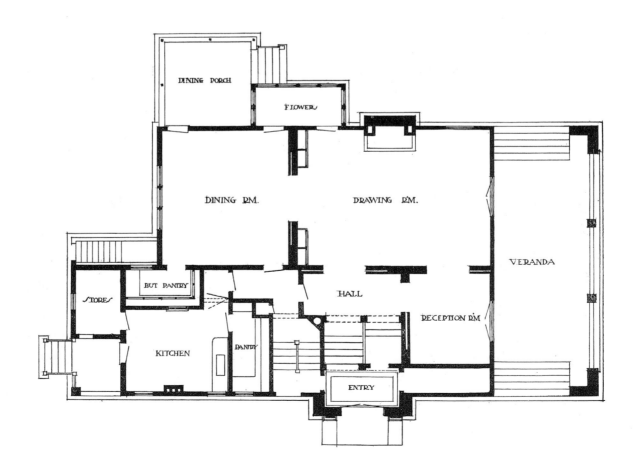

RESIDENCE OF J. F. BROWN, ZANESVILLE, OHIO J. P. Taylor, Architect

Stucco on Metal Lath

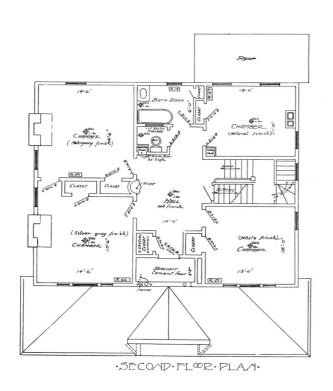

·SECOND·FLOOR·PLAN·

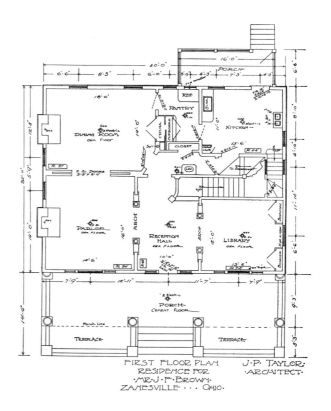

FIRST FLOOR PLAN J·P·TAYLOR·
RESIDENCE FOR ·ARCHITECT·
·MR·J·F·BROWN·
ZANESVILLE · · · OHIO·

RESIDENCE OF WALTER MITCHELL, MOBILE, ALA.
Stucco on Metal Lath

Stone Bros., Architects

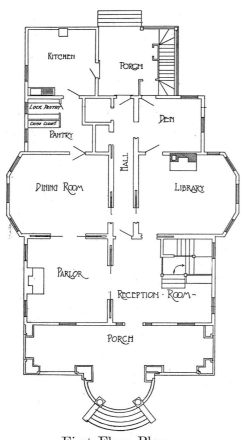

First Floor Plan

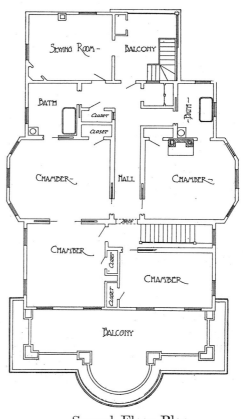

Second Floor Plan

RESIDENCE OF CHAS. DE WITT, BALTIMORE, MD.
Stucco on Brick

Ellicott & Emmart, Architects

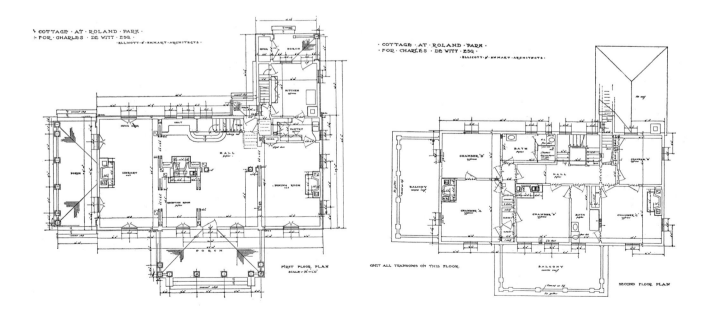

RESIDENCE OF F. C. BISHOP, TOLEDO, OHIO   A. W. Johnson, Architect
Stucco on Metal Lath

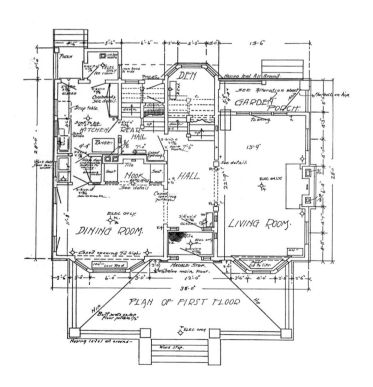

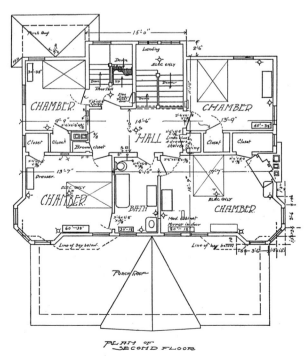

RESIDENCE OF R. P. GRAHAM, BALTIMORE, MD.   Ellicott & Emmart, Architects
Stucco on Metal Lath

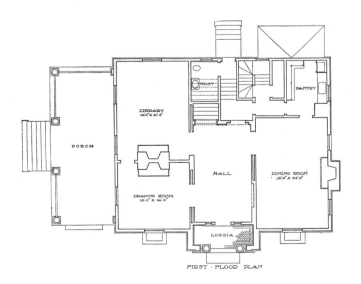

FIRST · FLOOR · PLAN

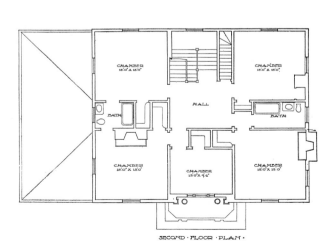

SECOND · FLOOR · PLAN

RESIDENCE OF L. B. REEDER, BALTIMORE, MD.   Ellicott & Emmart, Architects
Stucco on Metal Lath

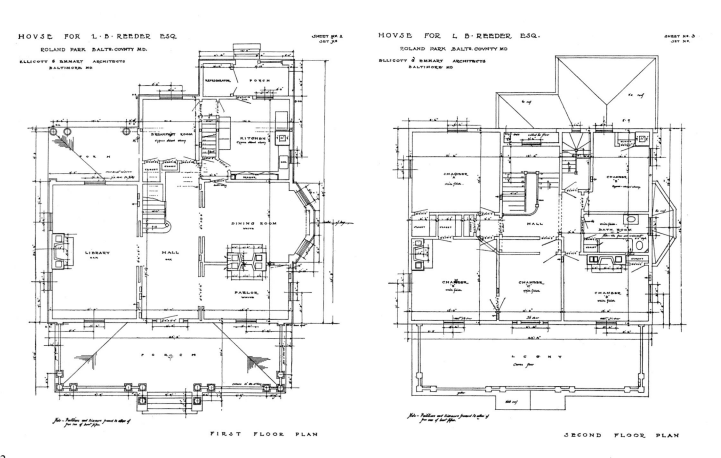

FIRST FLOOR PLAN   SECOND FLOOR PLAN

RESIDENCE OF H. T. HARTWELL, MOBILE, ALA.
Stucco on Metal Lath

Geo. B. Rogers, Architect

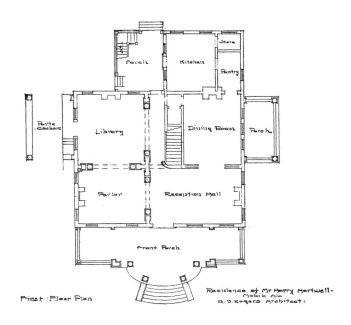

First Floor Plan

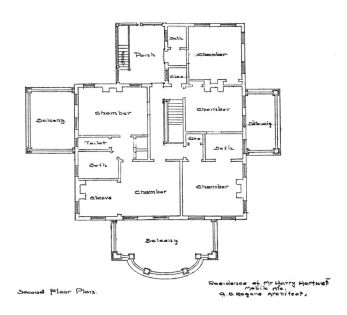

Second Floor Plan

RESIDENCE OF E. J. BUCK, MOBILE, ALA.   Geo. B. Rogers, Architect

Stucco on Brick

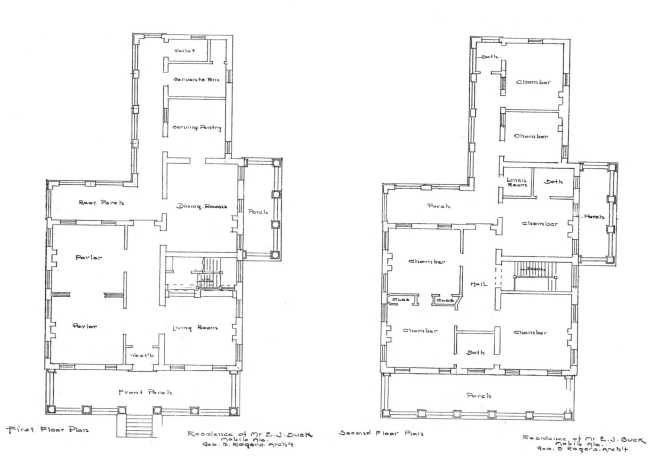

RESIDENCE OF DOMINICK DIETRICH, FT. THOMAS, KY.
Solid Reinforced Concrete

Gordon Sheppard, Architect

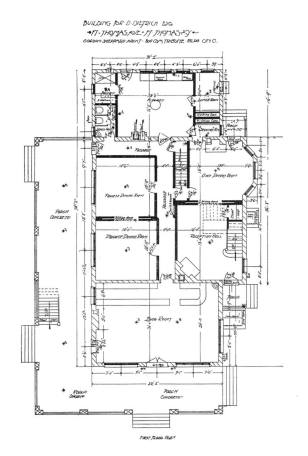

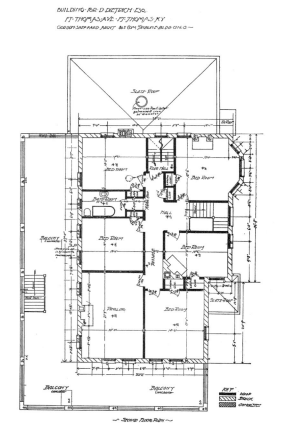

RESIDENCE OF J. R. WARE, FT. THOMAS, KY. Gordon Sheppard, Architect
Solid Reinforced Concrete

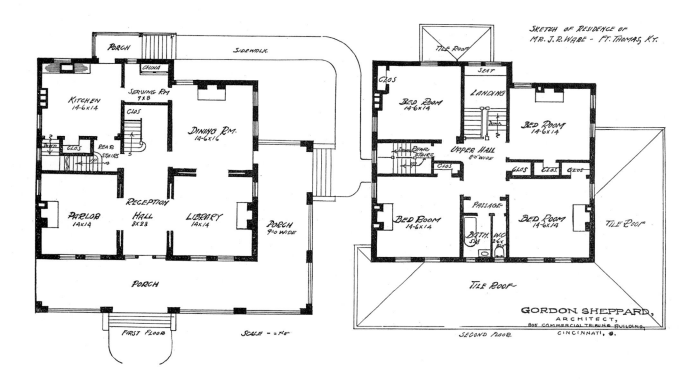

RESIDENCE OF MRS. J. E. JAMES, MONTCLAIR, N. J.   A. F. Norris, Architect
Stucco on Metal Lath

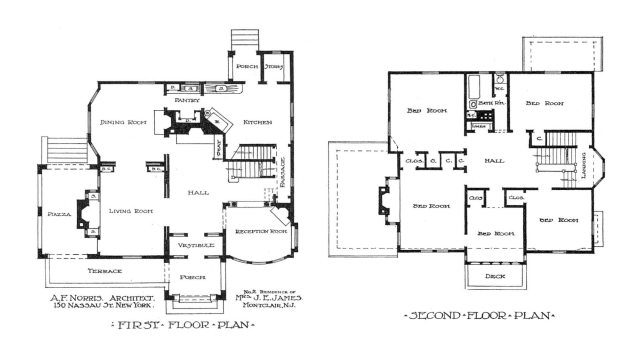

A. F. NORRIS, ARCHITECT.   No.2 RESIDENCE OF
150 NASSAU ST. NEW YORK.   MRS. J. E. JAMES.
                                  MONTCLAIR, N.J.

·FIRST·FLOOR·PLAN·   ·SECOND·FLOOR·PLAN·

RESIDENCE OF H. FENN, MONTCLAIR, N. J.   D. S. Van Antwerp, Architect
Stucco on Metal Lath

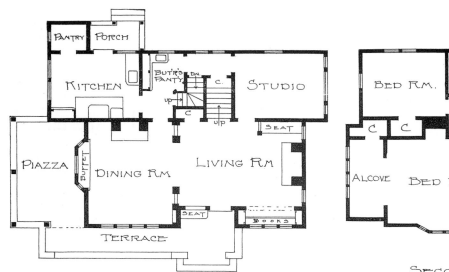

FIRST FLOOR PLAN

DUDLEY S. VAN ANTWERP, ARCH'T,
HILDA FENN VAN ANTWERP ASSOC.

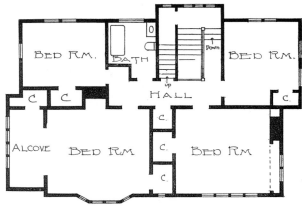

SECOND FLOOR PLAN

DUDLEY S. VAN ANTWERP ARCH'T,
HILDA FENN VAN ANTWERP ASSOC

RESIDENCE OF A. E. WUPPERMANN, MONTCLAIR, N. J.   A. F. Norris, Architect
Stucco on Metal Lath

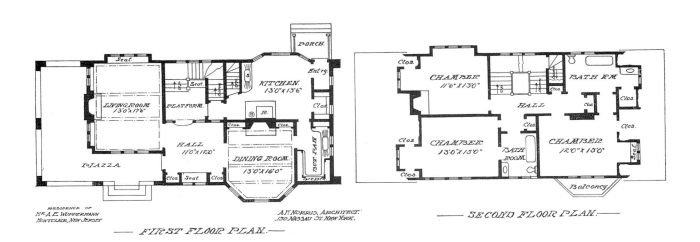

— FIRST FLOOR PLAN. —   — SECOND FLOOR PLAN. —

RESIDENCE OF MISS MARION HUBBARD, MONTCLAIR, N. J.   Van Vleck & Goldsmith, Architects
Stucco on Metal Lath

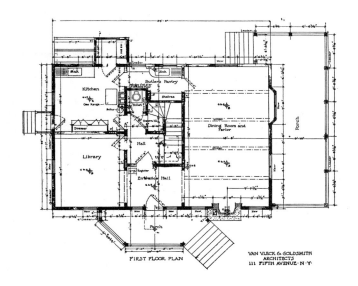

FIRST FLOOR PLAN   VAN VLECK & GOLDSMITH
ARCHITECTS
111 FIFTH AVENUE · N·Y·

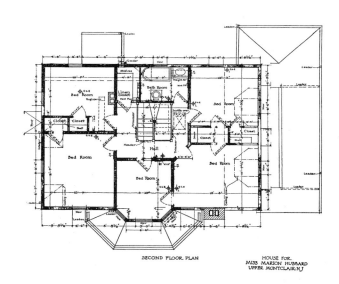

SECOND FLOOR PLAN   HOUSE FOR
MISS MARION HUBBARD
UPPER MONTCLAIR.N·J

RESIDENCE OF E. F. YOUMANS, NEW ROCHELLE, N. Y.   W. K. Benedict, Architect
Rubble and Stucco Concrete

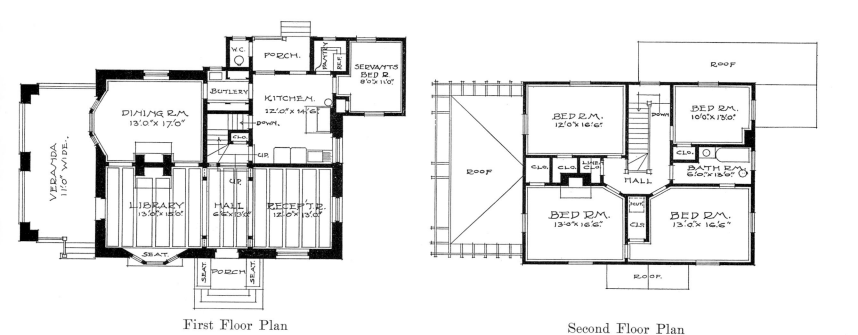

First Floor Plan   Second Floor Plan

RESIDENCE OF A. S. GROSSMANN, MONTCLAIR, N. J.   A. F. Norris, Architect
Stucco on Metal Lath

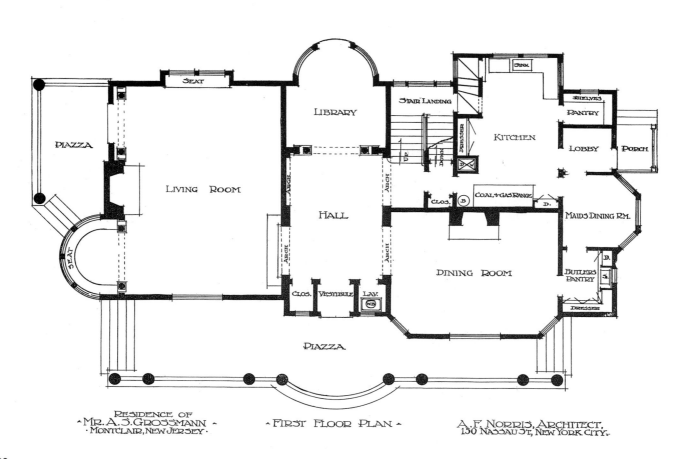

RESIDENCE OF
· MR. A. S. GROSSMANN ·
· MONTCLAIR, NEW JERSEY ·   · FIRST FLOOR PLAN ·   A. F. NORRIS, ARCHITECT,
130 NASSAU ST., NEW YORK CITY.

RESIDENCE OF F. H. JONES, MONTCLAIR, N. J.   A. F. Norris, Architect
Stucco on Metal Lath

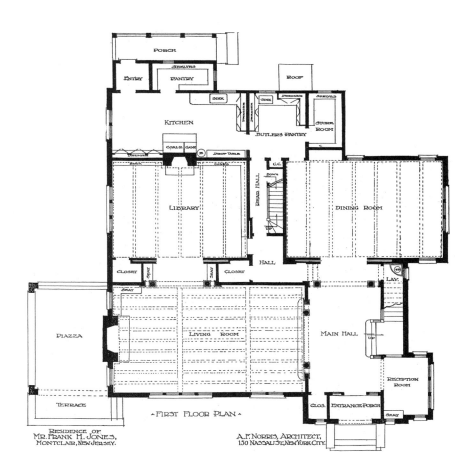

~ FIRST FLOOR PLAN ~

RESIDENCE OF
MR. FRANK H. JONES,
MONTCLAIR, NEW JERSEY.

A. F. NORRIS, ARCHITECT,
150 NASSAU ST., NEW YORK CITY.

RESIDENCE OF GEO. BATTEN, MONTCLAIR, N. J.   D. S. Van Antwerp, Architect
Stucco on Metal Lath

FIRST FLOOR PLAN   SECOND FLOOR PLAN

RESIDENCE OF D. S. VAN ANTWERP, MONTCLAIR, N. J.
Stucco on Metal Lath

D. S. Van Antwerp, Architect

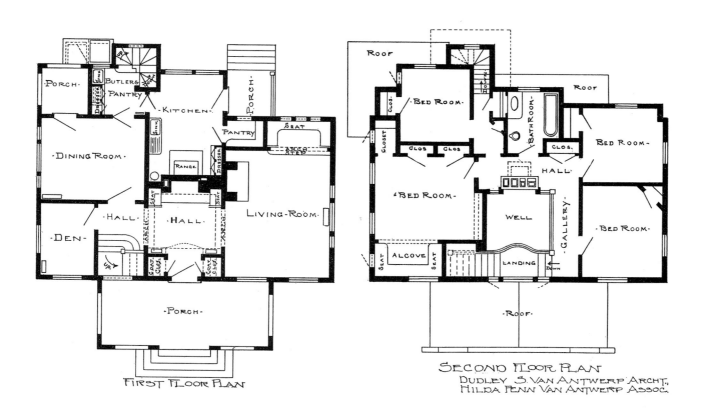

FIRST FLOOR PLAN

SECOND FLOOR PLAN
DUDLEY S. VAN ANTWERP ARCHT.
HILDA PENN VAN ANTWERP ASSOC.

RESIDENCE OF MRS. J. E. JAMES, MONTCLAIR, N. J. A. F. Norris, Architect
Stucco on Metal Lath

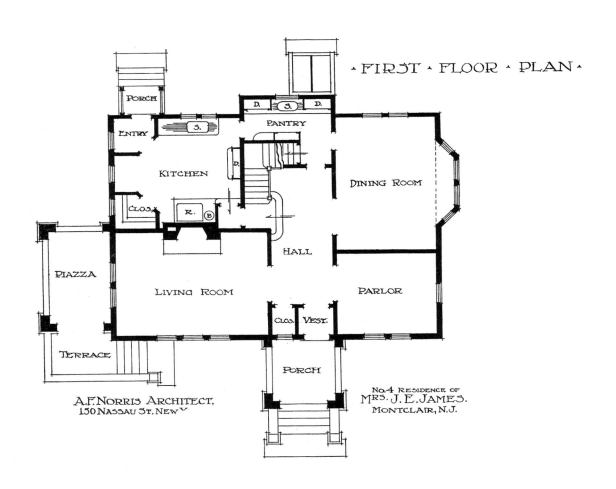

· FIRST · FLOOR · PLAN ·

PORCH

ENTRY

D. S. D.

PANTRY

KITCHEN

DINING ROOM

D.

CLOS.

R. B.

HALL

PIAZZA

LIVING ROOM

PARLOR

CLOS. VEST.

TERRACE

PORCH

A. F. NORRIS ARCHITECT,
150 NASSAU ST. NEW Y

No. 4 RESIDENCE OF
MRS. J. E. JAMES.
MONTCLAIR, N. J.

RESIDENCE OF ROBT. ANDERSON, CINCINNATI, OHIO
Solid Reinforced Concrete

Elzner & Anderson, Architects

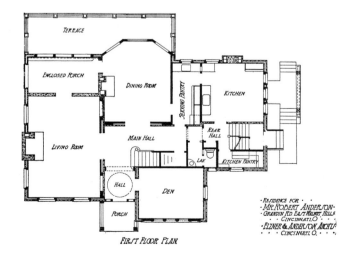

FIRST FLOOR PLAN

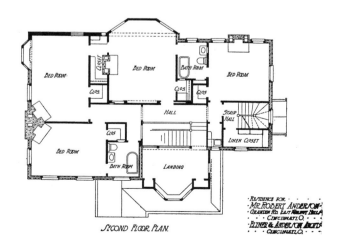

SECOND FLOOR PLAN

RESIDENCE OF SUMNER B. PEARMAIN, FRAMINGHAM, MASS.   Designed by Mrs. Sumner B. Pearmain
Built by Benj. A. Howes, Engineer
Solid Reinforced Concrete

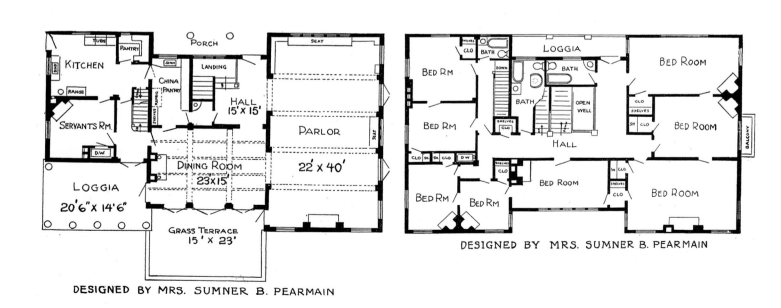

DESIGNED BY MRS. SUMNER B. PEARMAIN

DESIGNED BY MRS. SUMNER B. PEARMAIN

RESIDENCE OF M. F. GRIGGS, ARDSLEY-ON-THE-HUDSON, N. Y.

Robt. W. Gardner, Architect
Benj. A. Howes, Engineer

Solid Reinforced Concrete

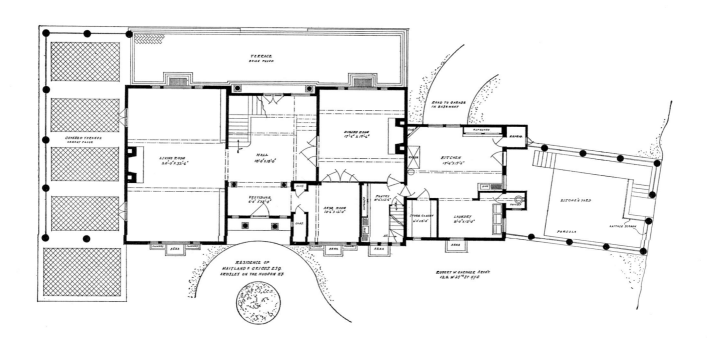

RESIDENCE OF ALEX. S. COCHRAN, EASTVIEW, N. Y.
Solid Reinforced Concrete

Robt. W. Gardner, Architect
Benj. A. Howes, Engineer

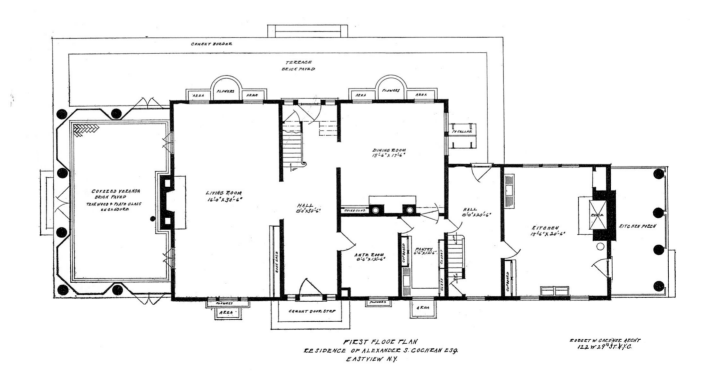

FIRST FLOOR PLAN
RESIDENCE OF ALEXANDER S. COCHRAN ESQ.
EASTVIEW N.Y.

RESIDENCE AT BRIARCLIFF MANOR, N. Y.   Arthur G. C. Fletcher, Architect
Solid Reinforced Concrete

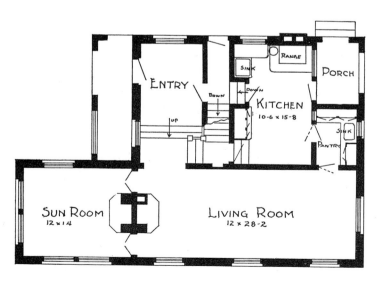

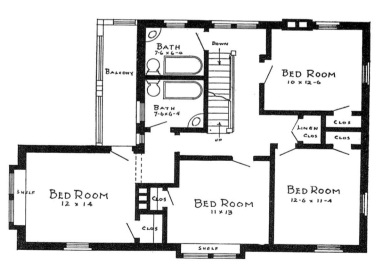

FIRST FLOOR PLAN   SECOND FLOOR PLAN

ARTHUR G. C. FLETCHER, ARCH'T
1133 BROADWAY. N.Y.

RESIDENCE OF H. B. GROSE, BRIARCLIFF MANOR, N. Y.   A. G. Richardson, Architect
Solid Reinforced Concrete

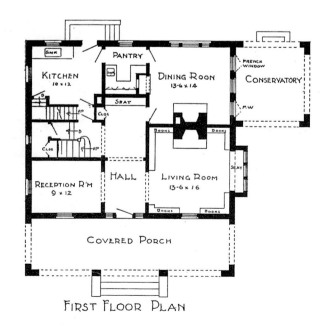

FIRST FLOOR PLAN

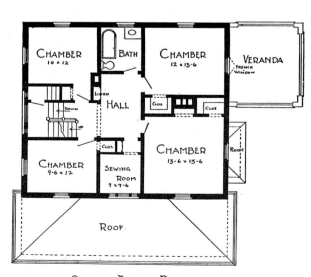

SECOND FLOOR PLAN

RESIDENCE OF PROF. B. ROBINSON, CAMBRIDGE, MASS.
Stucco on Metal Lath

Chas. K. Cummings, Architect

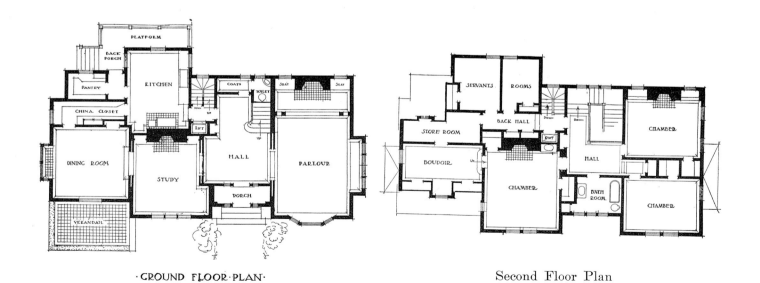

·GROUND FLOOR·PLAN·   Second Floor Plan

RESIDENCE OF MAURICE HOOPES, GLENS FALLS, N. Y.   Winslow & Bigelow, Architects
Stucco on Metal Lath

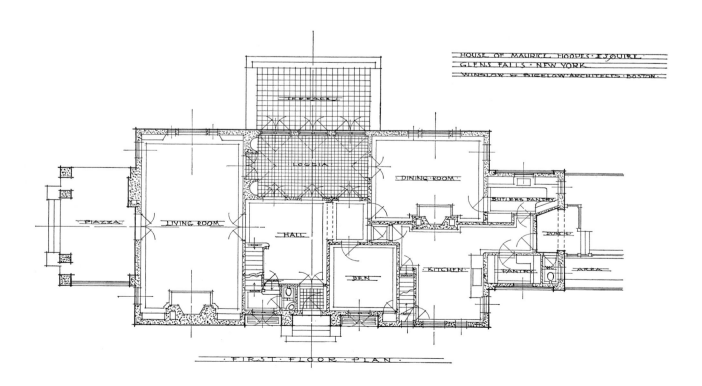

HOUSE OF MAURICE HOOPES ESQUIRE
GLENS FALLS · NEW YORK
WINSLOW & BIGELOW ARCHITECTS · BOSTON·

· FIRST · FLOOR · PLAN ·

RESIDENCE OF GEO. FEARN, JR., MOBILE, ALA.
Stucco on Metal Lath

Geo. B. Rogers, Architect

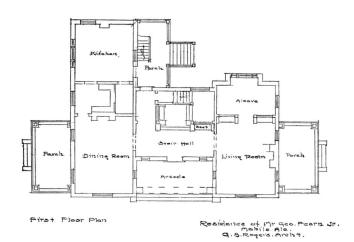

First Floor Plan

Residence of Mr Geo. Fearn Jr.
Mobile Ala.
G. B. Rogers. Arch't.

Second Floor Plan

Residence of Mr Geo Fearn Jr.
Mobile Ala
G. B. Rogers. Arch't.

RESIDENCE OF C. Y. TUCKER, NEW DORP, S. I.   Robt. W. Gardner, Architect
Hollow Concrete Blocks

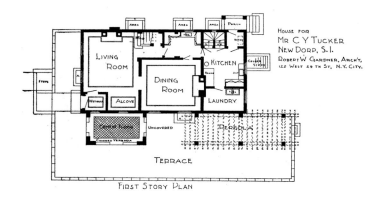

FIRST STORY PLAN

SECOND STORY PLAN

RESIDENCE OF L. W. HAIGHT, WHITE PLAINS, N. Y.   Hans Hilton, Architect
Solid Reinforced Concrete

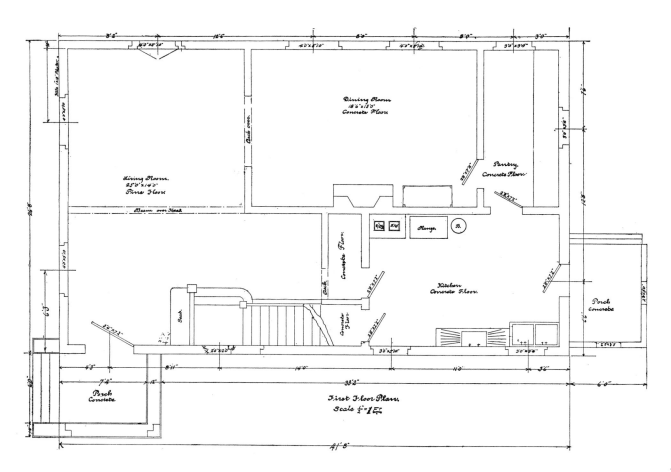

RESIDENCE OF MISS FRANCES MACDANIEL, GARDEN CITY, L. I.
Solid Reinforced Concrete

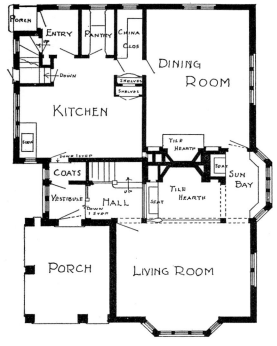

PLAN OF FIRST FLOOR

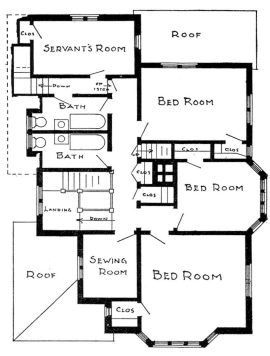

PLAN OF SECOND FLOOR

RESIDENCE OF BASSETT JONES, YONKERS, N. Y.   S. W. Jones, Architect
Solid Reinforced Concrete

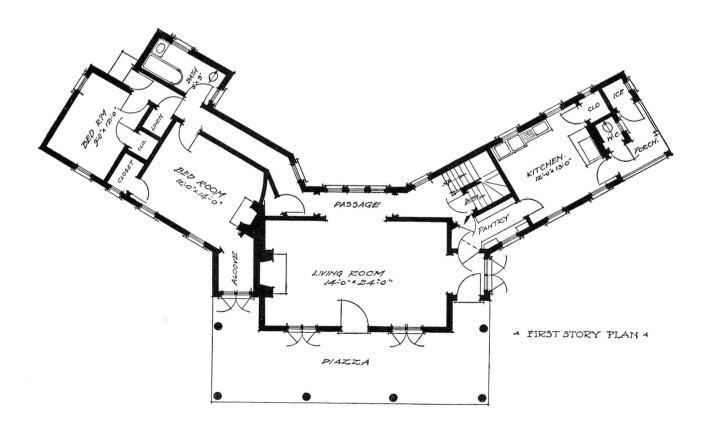

FIRST STORY PLAN

BUNGALOW AT HAWORTH, N. J.   Bayard Wight, Architect

Solid Reinforced Concrete

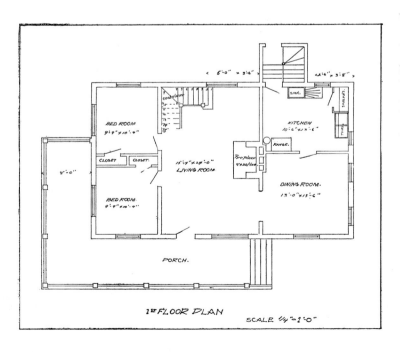

1ST FLOOR PLAN   SCALE ¼"=1'-0"

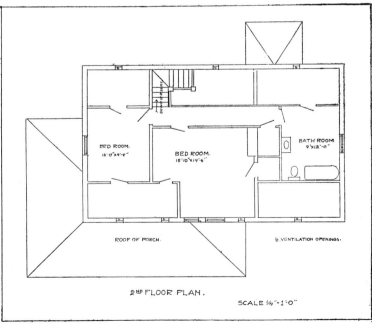

2ND FLOOR PLAN.   SCALE ¼"=1'-0"

RESIDENCE OF WM. R. FISH, HAWORTH, N. J.
Solid Concrete Blocks

A. C. Pauli, Architect

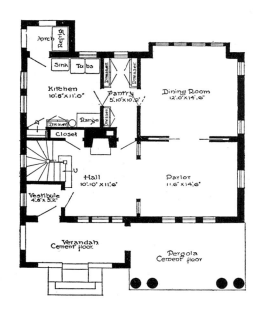

·PLAN OF FIRST FLOOR·

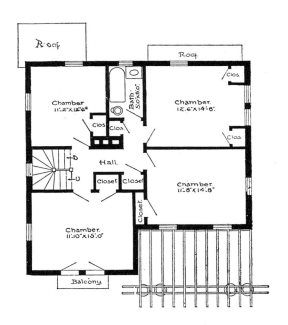

·PLAN OF SECOND FLOOR·

RESIDENCE AT HAWORTH, N. J.   Fred. Robbin, Jr., Architect

Solid Reinforced Concrete

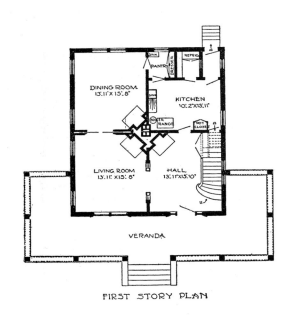

FIRST STORY PLAN

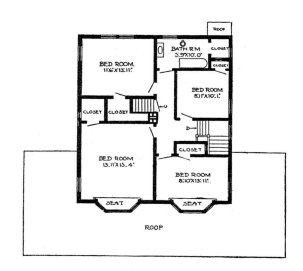

SECOND STORY PLAN

RESIDENCE OF PAUL G. HENNING, HAWORTH, N. J.   A. C. Pauli, Architect
Solid Reinforced Concrete

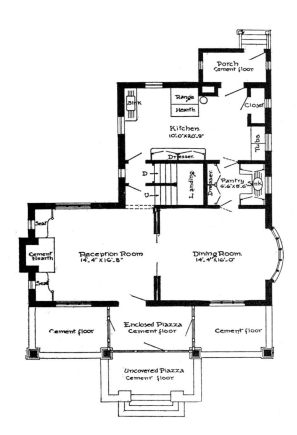

PLAN OF FIRST FLOOR

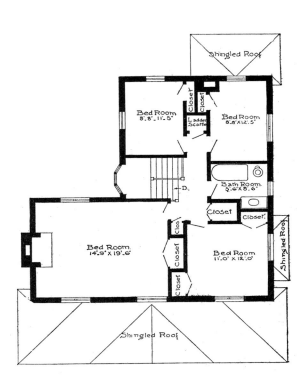

PLAN OF SECOND FLOOR

RESIDENCE OF R. D. ADDIS, HAWORTH, N. J.   A. C. Pauli, Architect
Solid Reinforced Concrete

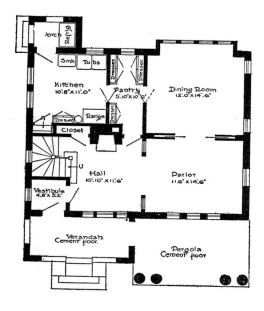

·PLAN OF FIRST FLOOR·

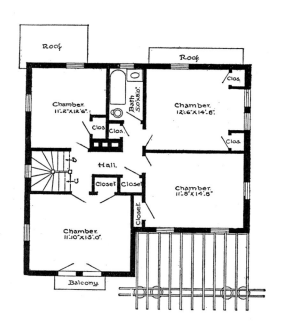

·PLAN OF SECOND FLOOR·

RESIDENCE OF H. R. RODEN, HAWORTH, N. J.
Solid Concrete Block Construction

Fred. Robbin, Jr., Architect

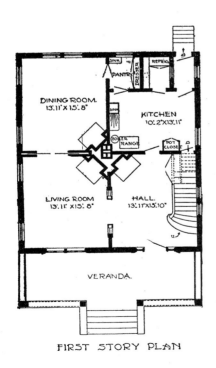

FIRST STORY PLAN

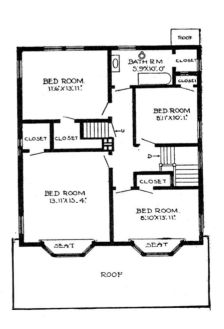

SECOND STORY PLAN

RESIDENCE OF C. C. VAN ALSTEIN, OCONOMOWOC, WIS.   John Menge, Jr., Architect
Solid Reinforced Concrete

FIRST FLOOR PLAN
J. MENGE JR ARCHT.

BASEMENT PLAN.
J. MENGE JR ARCHT.

RESIDENCE OF S. E. GARD, SIOUX CITY, IOWA   P. P. Comoli, Architect and Builder
Solid Reinforced Concrete

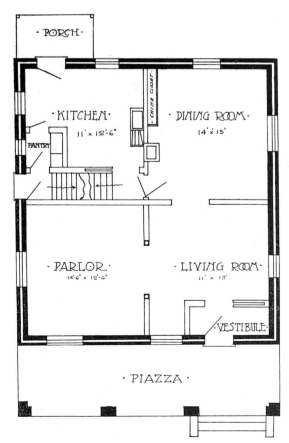

First Floor Plan

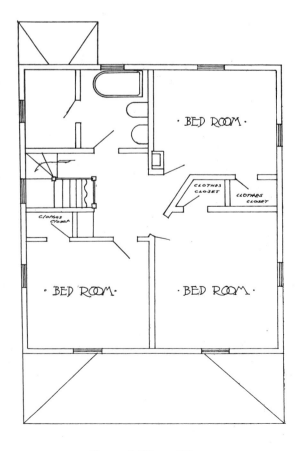

Second Floor Plan

RESIDENCE OF W. S. HOOLE, SIOUX CITY, IOWA   P. P. Comoli, Architect and Builder
Solid Reinforced Concrete

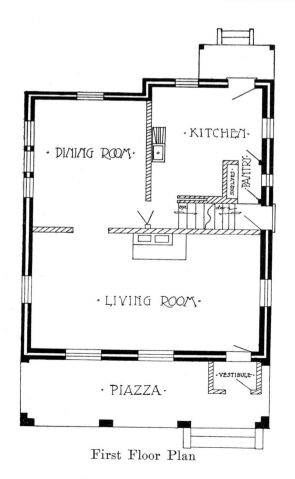

First Floor Plan

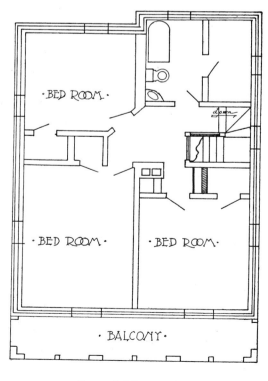

Second Floor Plan

Residence of W. B. Gibbons, Sioux City, Iowa   P. P. Comoli, Architect and Builder
Solid Reinforced Concrete

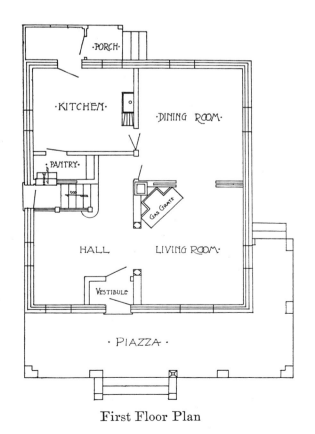

First Floor Plan

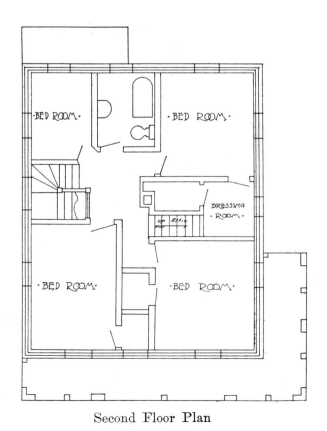

Second Floor Plan

RESIDENCE OF P. P. COMOLI, SIOUX CITY, IOWA   P. P. Comoli, Architect and Builder
Solid Reinforced Concrete

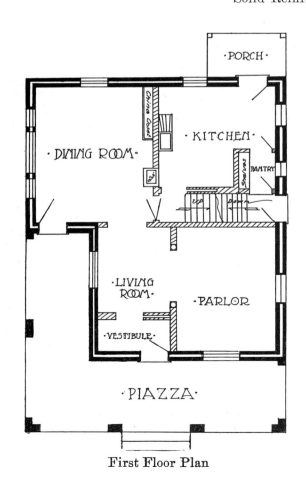

First Floor Plan   Second Floor Plan

RESIDENCE OF HENRY DANZIGER, JR., SYRACUSE, N. Y.   G. A. Wright, Architect
Stucco on Brick

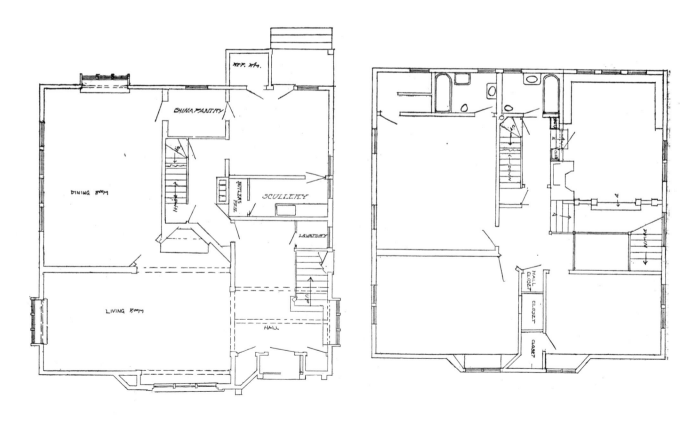

FIRST FLOOR PLAN
SCALE ⅛"=1'

SECOND FLOOR PLAN
SCALE ⅛"=1'

RESIDENCE OF PAUL E. SEARLES, EAST CLEVELAND, OHIO   Searles, Hirsh & Gavin, Architects
Stucco on Metal Lath

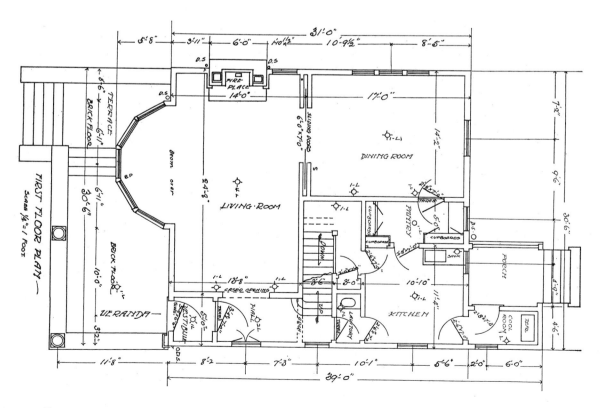

HOUSE ON ROSEMONT ROAD.
SEARLES · HIRSH · & GAVIN
— ARCHITECTS —

RESIDENCE OF M. S. HOTCHKISS, LESTERSHIRE, N. Y.
Solid Reinforced Concrete

Gardner & Bartoo, Architects

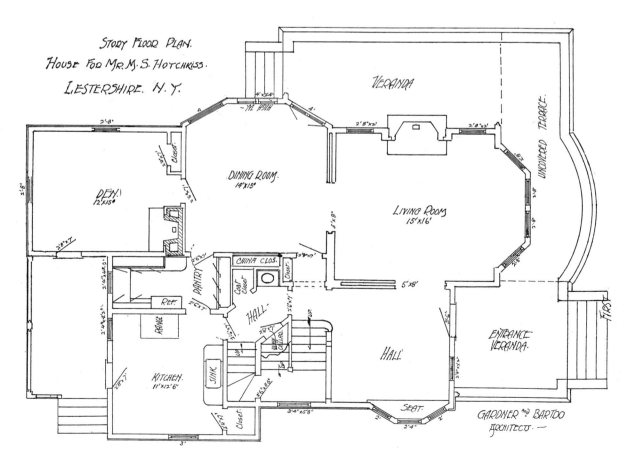

STORY FLOOR PLAN.
HOUSE FOR MR. M. S. HOTCHKISS.
LESTERSHIRE. N. Y.

VERANDA

UNCOVERED TERRACE.

DINING ROOM.
14'x15'

LIVING ROOM
15'x16'

DEN.
12'x15'

CHINA CLOS.

PANTRY

Coat Closet

Closet

REF.

HALL

5'x8'

RANGE

HALL

ENTRANCE
VERANDA.

KITCHEN.
11'x12'6"

SINK

SEAT.

GARDNER AND BARTOO
ARCHITECTS.

RESIDENCE OF P. C. JONES, TOLEDO, OHIO   B. Becker, Architect
Stucco on Metal Lath

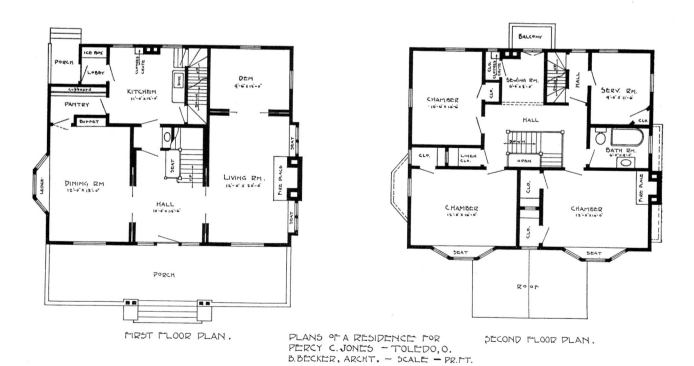

FIRST FLOOR PLAN.   PLANS OF A RESIDENCE FOR   SECOND FLOOR PLAN.
                           PERCY C. JONES — TOLEDO, O.
                           B. BECKER, ARCHT. — SCALE — PR. FT.

BEACONSFIELD HOTEL, BROOKLINE, MASS.   Fehmer & Page, Architects
Stucco on Brick

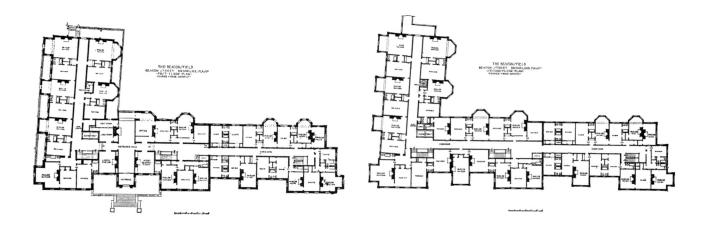

IVANHOE APARTMENTS, ALLSTON, MASS.   C. H. Blackall, Architect
Reinforced Concrete with Block Walls

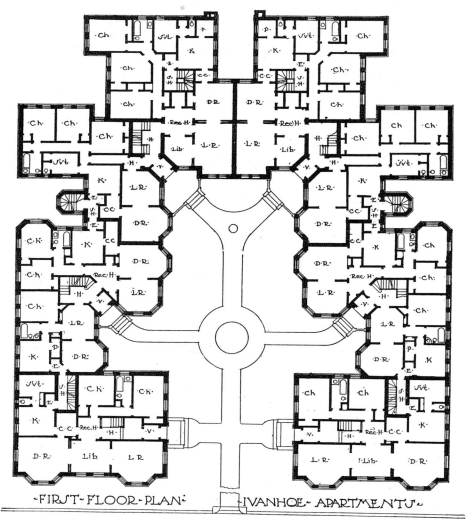

·FIRST·FLOOR·PLAN·   ·IVANHOE·APARTMENTS·

GARDNER STREET.

APARTMENTS AT 137TH STREET AND RIVERSIDE DRIVE, N. Y. C.
Solid Reinforced Concrete   L. C. Maurer, Architect

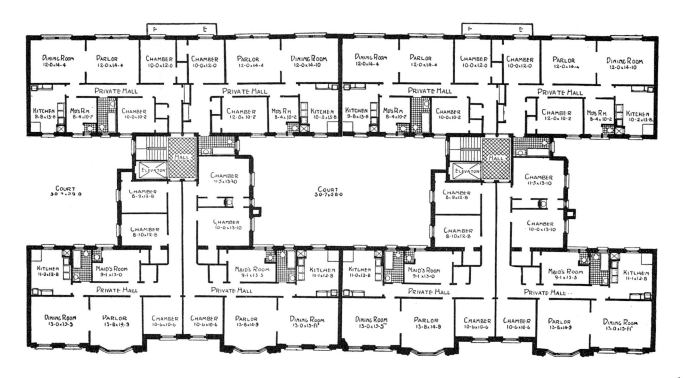

HOLLENBECK HOME FOR AGED PEOPLE, LOS ANGELES, CAL.   Morgan & Walls, Architects

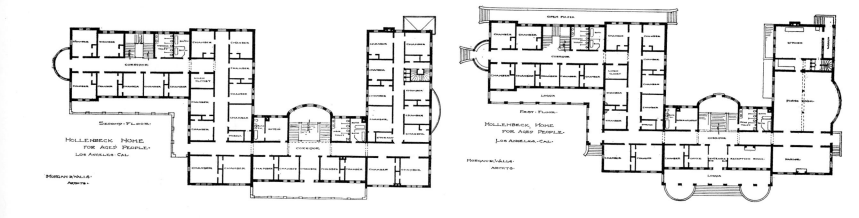

DORMITORY AT COLD SPRING HARBOR, L. I.
Solid Reinforced Concrete

Gardner & Howes, Architects

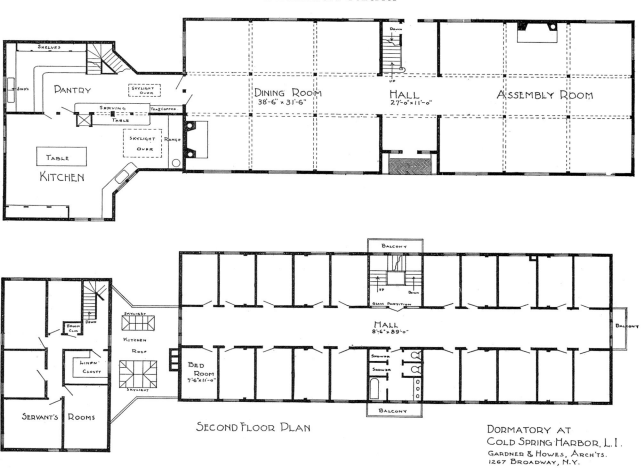

SECOND FLOOR PLAN

DORMATORY AT
COLD SPRING HARBOR, L. I.
GARDNER & HOWES, ARCH'TS.
1267 BROADWAY, N.Y.

RIVERSIDE SHELTER HOUSE, INDIANAPOLIS, IND.　　　　Clyde Power, Architect
Solid Reinforced Concrete

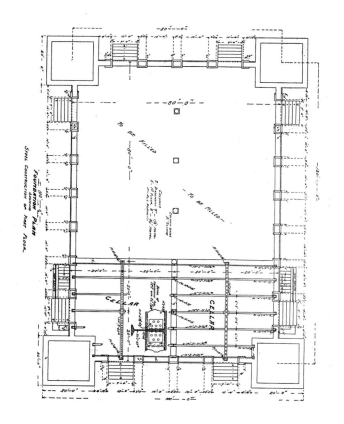

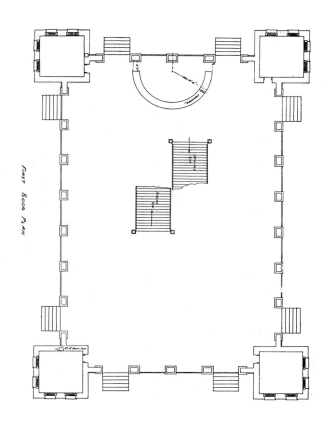

Neighborhood Club House, Sherman Park, Chicago, Ill.   D. H. Burnham & Co., Architects
Solid Reinforced Concrete

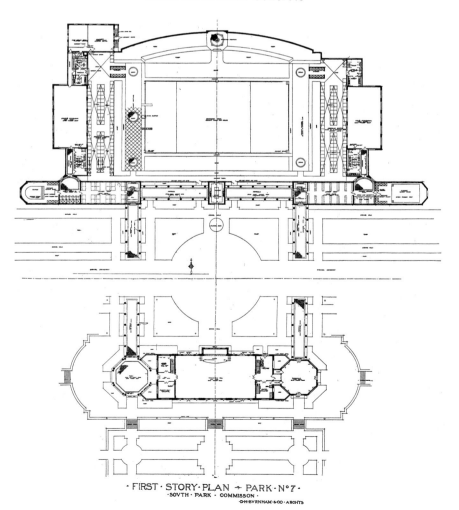

· FIRST · STORY · PLAN ✦ PARK · Nº 7 ·
· SOVTH · PARK · COMMISSON ·
· D·H·BVRNHAM·&·CO · ARCHTS

COUNTRY CLUB HOUSE, WALNUT HILLS, CINCINNATI, OHIO   Elzner & Anderson, Architects
Stucco on Metal Lath

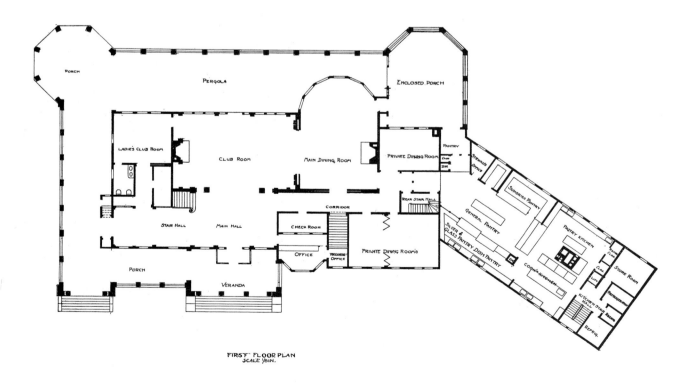

FIRST FLOOR PLAN
SCALE ⅛IN.

CLUB HOUSE FOR COUNTRY CLUB
GRANDIN ROAD EAST WALNUT HILLS
ELZNER & ANDERSON ARCHITECTS CIN. O

THE BOAT HOUSE OF THE DETROIT BOAT CLUB, DETROIT, MICH.   A. W. Chittenden, Architect
Stucco on Brick

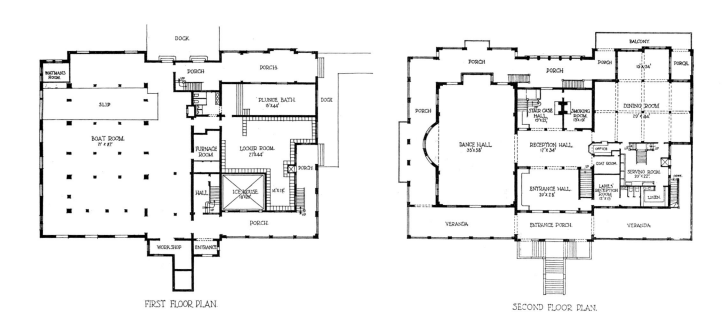

FIRST FLOOR PLAN.   SECOND FLOOR PLAN.

STABLE OF F. L. STETSON, STERLINGTON, N. Y.   Alfred Hopkins, Architect
Solid Reinforced Concrete

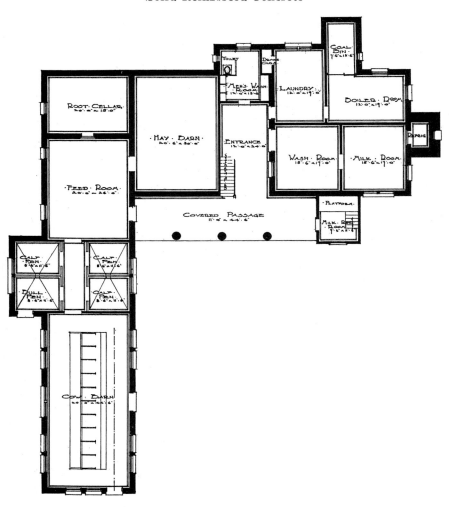

STABLE OF F. F. PALMER, PORTCHESTER, N. Y.

F. H. Dodge, Architect
Pottier & Stymus Co., Consulting Architects
Stucco on Metal Lath

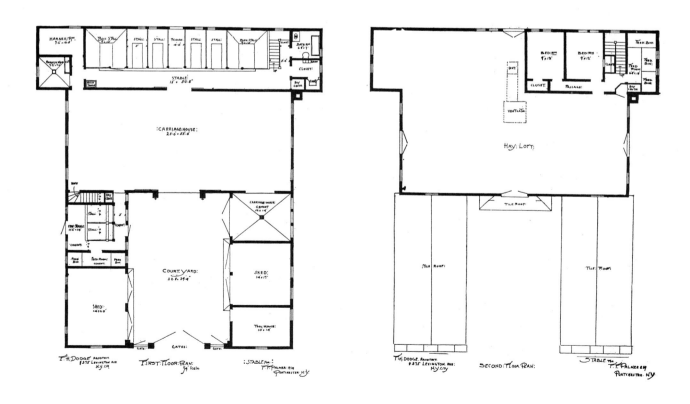

STABLE OF N. F. PALMER, PORTCHESTER, N. Y.
F. H. Dodge, Architect
Pottier & Stymus Co., Consulting Architects
Stucco on Metal Lath

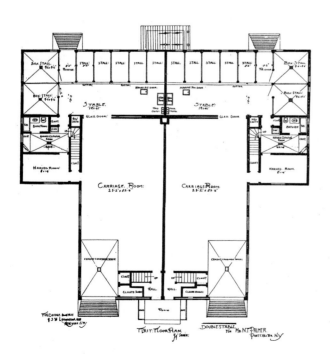

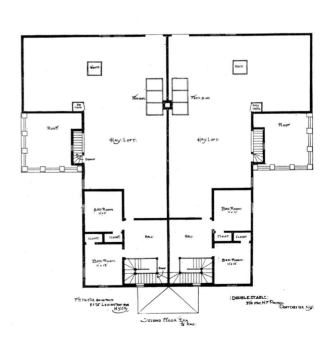

STABLE AT THE RESIDENCE OF W. D. DENEGRE, Andrews, Jaques & Rantoul, Architects
MANCHESTER, MASS. Stucco on Metal Lath

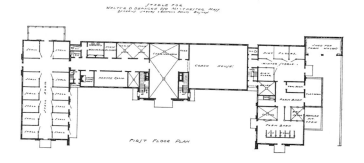

STABLE OF C. S. HOUGHTON, CHESTNUT HILL, MASS.
Stucco on Metal Lath

Chapman & Frazer, Architects

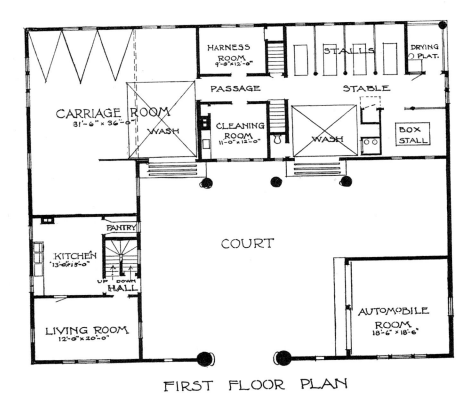

HARNESS ROOM
9'-0"x12'-0"

STALLS

DRYING PLAT.

PASSAGE

STABLE

CARRIAGE ROOM
31'-6" x 36'-0"

WASH

CLEANING ROOM
11'-0" x 12'-0"

WASH

BOX STALL

COURT

PANTRY

KITCHEN
13'-0"x15'-0"

UP DOWN
HALL

AUTOMOBILE ROOM
18'-6" x 18'-6"

LIVING ROOM
12'-0" x 20'-0"

FIRST FLOOR PLAN

STABLE AT CHESTNUT HILL MASS
CHAPMAN & FRAZER ARCHTS BOSTON

STABLE OF DR. N. B. VAN ETTEN, NEW YORK CITY   Robt. W. Gardner, Architect
Solid Reinforced Concrete

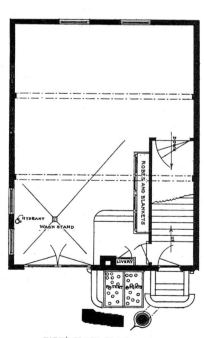

FIRST FLOOR PLAN
STABLE OF DR. N.B. VANETTEN.

ROBERT W. GARDNER ARCHT
1347 BROADWAY N.Y.C.

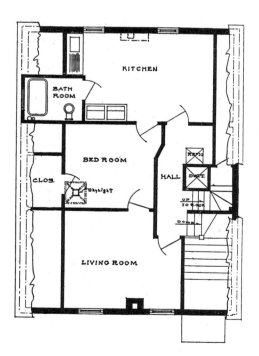

SECOND FLOOR PLAN
STABLE OF DR.N.B. VANETTEN

ROBERT W.GARDNER ARCH'T.
1347 BROADWAY N.Y.C.

MOTOR HOUSE FOR A. S. COCHRAN, TARRYTOWN, N. Y.   Gardner & Howes, Architects
Rubble Concrete

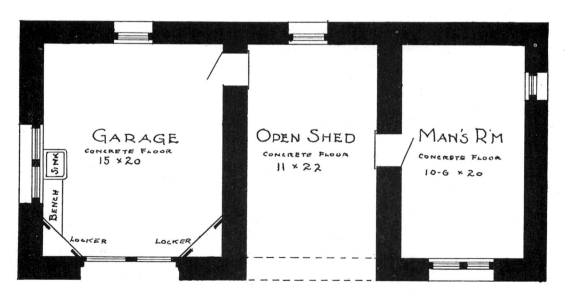

MOTOR HOUSE FOR
MR. ALEXANDER S. COCHRAN
TARRYTOWN, N.Y.

GARDNER AND HOWES
1267 BROADWAY N.Y.
ARCHITECTS AND ENGINEERS

GARAGE OF JONATHAN THORNE, BLACK ROCK, CONN.
Solid Reinforced Concrete

Gardner & Howes, Architects

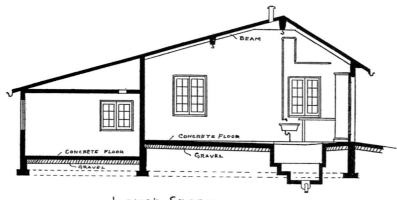

LONG'L SECTION

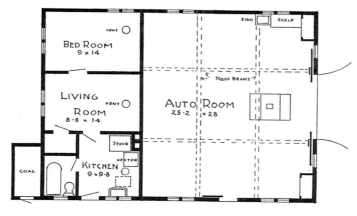

GROUND PLAN

REINFORCED CONCRETE GARAGE FOR
JONATHAN THORNE ESQ
BLACK ROCK, CONN.

GARDNER AND HOWES
1267 BROADWAY N.Y.
ARCHITECTS

141

WORKINGMEN'S HOUSES, PALMERTON, PA.   M. T. J. Ochs, Builder
Stucco on Metal Lath
Blocks of Four.—Front View

Rear View

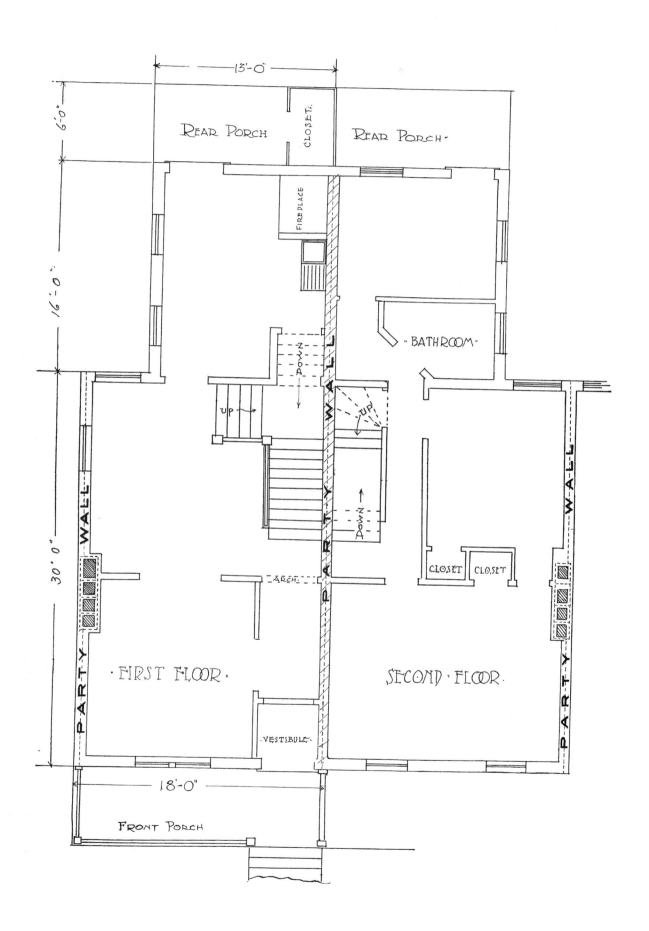

WORKINGMEN'S HOUSES, PALMERTON, PA.   M. T. J. Ochs, Builder
Stucco on Metal Lath
Blocks of Two.—Front View

Rear View

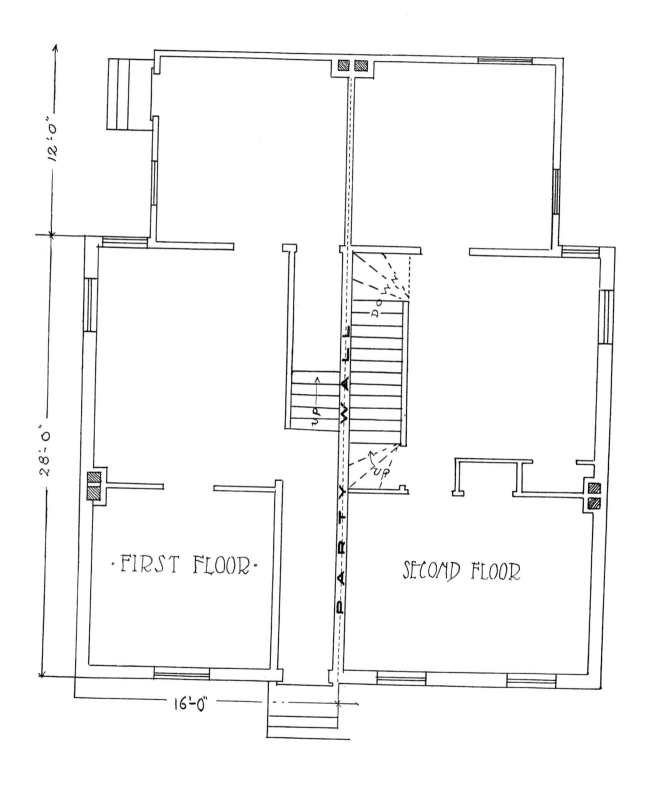

WORKINGMEN'S HOUSES, MILWAUKEE, WIS.
Solid Reinforced Concrete

Louis Auer & Sons, Architects

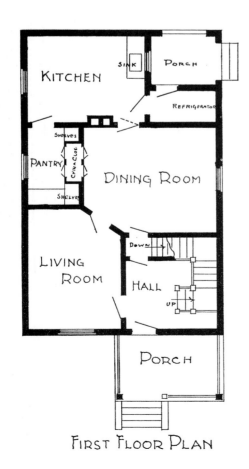

FIRST FLOOR PLAN

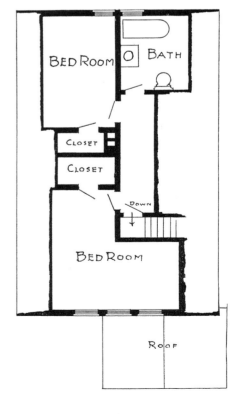

SECOND FLOOR PLAN

A COMPETITION FOR SUBURBAN HOUSES IN CONCRETE

First Prize—Eugene Ward, Jr., Architect, 11 East Twenty-fourth Street, New York

FIRST FLOOR PLAN

LIVING ROOM 13'4" x 19'4"
KITCHEN 9'0"x9'4"
PANTRY
PORCH 5'0"x9'0"
HALL 4'6"x11'5"
PORCH 8'0"x15'0"
ENTRY
DINING TABLE
SCREEN

SECOND FLOOR PLAN

BED ROOM 9'x13'4"
BED ROOM 9'x13'4"
BATH ROOM
CLOS.
LINEN
HALL
IRON BALCONIES

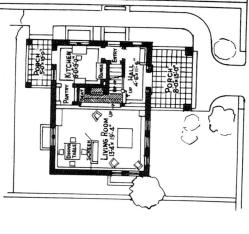

CROSS SECTION

STORY HEIGHTS – BASEMENT SEVEN FT., FIRST STORY NINE FT., SECOND STORY EIGHT FT., ALL CLEAR
OUTSIDE DIMENSIONS OF HOUSE TWENTY BY TWENTY-SEVEN.

Description: Outer walls and porch posts to be of monolithic concrete construction. Cellar and porch floors to be of concrete. Outer walls to be 8 inches thick, cemented on the outside and furred with wood furring strips and plastered on wood lath on the inside. Outside walls to have rough cast finish, stained. Chimneys to be lined with flue tile. Cellar under whole house.

All piers in basement, partitions on first floor, and main bearing partitions on upper floors to be of hollow cement blocks, plastered.

Floor joists 2 x 10 inch, 16-inch O.C. Rafters 2 x 6-inch. Minor partitions to be of 2 x 4-inch studs lathed and plastered. All floors double with hard pine upper floors. Trim to be cypress stained. Sash of white pine, painted. All glass D. S. A. Hardware of good grade. Fireplace of selected hard burned brick. Roofs shingled with red asbestos cement shingles. Balcony at second story front bedroom to be of 1/16-inch flat steel riveted and painted black.

ESTIMATE.

Excavation	$40.00
Concrete and cement work	890.00
Carpentry	355.00
Trim	450.00
Painting, etc.	80.00
Hardware	50.00
Tin work	30.00
Wiring, etc.	60.00
	$1,955.00

Cubic contents, 15,086 cubic feet, including porches.

COMMITTEE'S COMMENTS.

This design is most admirable, having a distinct, individual charm in both plan and elevation. This applies particularly to the arrangement of the entrance, stairs and living room. The use of a single chimney is economical, as is also the simple outline of the exterior walls, the recessed panels of which can be readily formed in monolithic construction by boards nailed to the inside of the forms. The drawings are exquisitely rendered. The specifications designate rough cast finish for the exterior walls. This is a questionable surface treatment for concrete, as plaster of any thickness is likely to peel from dampness and frost. However, the surface treatment might be readily modified.

A3 COMPETITION FOR SUBURBAN CONCRETE BUILDINGS

FIRST FLOOR PLAN

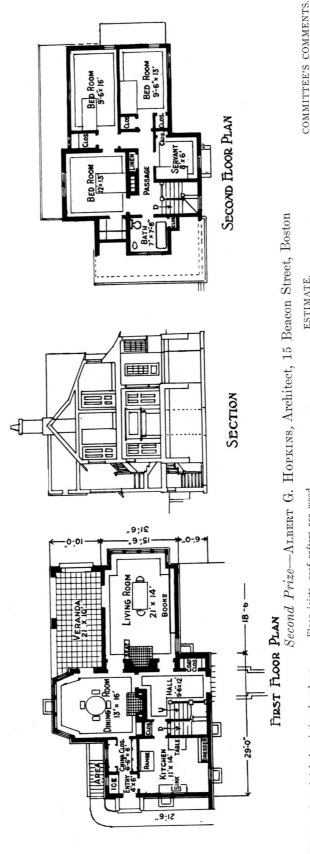

SECTION

SECOND FLOOR PLAN

The following is a brief description based on the enclosed estimate:

Foundation walls to be monolithic concrete—base above grade hammered.

Walls to be of plain-faced concrete blocks, 8 inches thick, 12 inches high, 12 inches, 24 inches and 30 inches long.

Veranda piers 12-inch blocks.

Floors of verandas and porches are cement finish concrete.

Blocks under eaves, front door hood and service wall coping to be of concrete.

Monolithic lintels over windows, reinforced.

Chimneys are brick, tile lined, plastered above roof, with cement cap and tile chimney pots.

Floor joists, roof rafters are wood. Roof shingles and stained-copper gutters and conductors.

Interior partitions are wood studded, plastered two coats.

Interior finish is cypress stained in living room, dining room and halls, white wood painted in bed-rooms and bath.

North Carolina pine finished natural in service portion.

Walls in bathroom and entire service portion painted with one coat shellac, three coats lead and oil.

Floors in living room, dining room and halls and stair rail and treads best quartered oak. Floors in service portion and entire second floor best rift hard pine.

Second Prize—ALBERT G. HOPKINS, Architect, 15 Beacon Street, Boston

ESTIMATE.

Excavating and brick work....................	$235.00
Concrete foundation, areas, etc.............	410.00
Concrete block walls.......................	445.00
Cement floors for porches.................	35.00
Lumber and shingles.......................	440.00
Finished fireplaces and mantels..........	100.00
Inside and outside finish and stairs.....	550.00
Finished floors...........................	100.00
Windows, doors and blinds.................	250.00
Plastering, inside and out................	375.00
Painting, inside and out..................	300.00
Carpenter labor...........................	600.00
	$3,840.00

Iron beams.
Cubic contents, 31,500 cubic feet.

COMMITTEE'S COMMENTS.

This design, while less simple in its lines than the "first prize" (shown on page 157) is as much a concrete block type as that is a monolithic. The plain surfaces are well broken. The floor plans, while less compact, are equally good, and the exterior is most pleasing and harmonious. The flues from the two fireplaces, the range and the furnace are drawn together into a simple stack. The drawings are beautifully presented.

FRONT ELEVATION.

LIVING ROOM END.

GARDEN ELEVATION.

A² Competition for Suburban Houses in Concrete

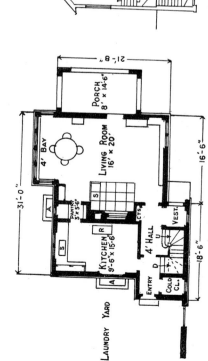

SECOND FLOOR PLAN

SECTION THRO' HALL AND LIVING ROOM

FIRST FLOOR PLAN

First Prize—ALBERT G. HOPKINS, Architect, 15 Beacon Street, Boston

The estimate is based on the following specifications:

The outside walls and vestibule to be of 8-inch hollow concrete blocks, plain face and light blue gray in color. The blocks show in vestibule, 12-inch monolithic foundation.

Monolithic lintels (waterproofed) with two square rods in bottom of lintel to be used over all openings. Granolithic porch floors, front and back door steps and living-room hearth marked off into 2-inch squares.

First and second floor walls and ceilings plastered, rough floated. (Except the living room and porch ceilings, which show the 2 x 6-inch joists and girders.) Porch ceiling to be left rough sawed.

Outside finish (of cypress), blinds, doors and

sash to be painted. Inside finish of cypress, waxed, except kitchen, which is to be shellaced. Kitchen and bathroom walls to be painted (oil paint) on smooth plaster. All other plaster walls throughout house to be tinted on rough floated plaster. Latches will be used on the outside doors and laundry yard gate.

The window frames set practically flush with the outside wall, giving a plaster reveal on the inside. The window frame and wooden stool form the inside finish for same.

All finish inside and outside to be plain—no moldings.

Inside doors to be four panel, stock pattern. North Carolina hard pine floors throughout. Laundry in basement. Shingle roof.

ESTIMATE.

8-inch blocks	$412.00
12-inch monolithic foundation	237.22
Granolithic	209.83
Excavating and mason work (apart from above work)	200.00
Plastering	250.00
Painting, staining and tinting	200.00
Gutters, conductors and hardware	40.00
Finished hardware	40.00
Windows and frames and weights and doors	200.00
Carpenter material and labor	1,000.00
Electric wiring	35.00
	$2,844.05

Cubic contents, 25,747 cubic feet.

COMMITTEE'S COMMENTS.

A concrete block design of excellent plan and charming exterior, beautifully rendered with a suggestion of its surroundings. The use of a single chimney is to be commended and the termination of the main wall construction at the general level of the eaves. The surfaces are well broken, already mentioned as desirable where blocks are used.

FIRST FLOOR PLAN ~ SECOND FLOOR PLAN

LONGITUDINAL SECTION

COMPETITION · FOR · SUBURBAN DWELLINGS · IN · CONCRETE

Third Prize—GRANT M. SIMON AND ABRAM BASTON, Architects, 1524 Chestnut Street, Philadelphia

Method of Construction: Monolithic construction will be used throughout the building, with the exception of partitions. The exterior walls will be of reinforced concrete 6 inches thick, furred inside 4 inches, with the rough lumber that was used in the forms.

Foundations: The foundations will be 9 inches of reinforced concrete, and will extend below the frost line where not excavated. Partitions in both will be of 3-inch concrete blocks, as suggested by programme. The forms will be of 5-inch slabs with necessary beams and girders. On all concrete floors will be a single wooden floor laid on sleepers beveled on top, spaces between filled with concrete.

The ceiling on the second floor will be furred down on metal lath.

Stairs and Cellar: The stairs will be of concrete with wooden treads and risers, with the exception of cellar stairs, which are to have cement finish. The cellar will extend only under the living room, and is to have a cement floor. It will

be lighted and ventilated by an area window on side of house.

Description: This scheme lends itself to the typical narrow suburban lot, with ample room on the side for gardens. The plan has been so arranged as to give large living room, kitchen, two bed-rooms and a bath.

In order to attain an interesting texture for the exterior walls, we suggest that while concrete is being placed in forms, the part next to the forms be pressed back with shovels, thus allowing the smaller stones and concrete to work their way to the front, giving a texture like pebble dash.

This method has been used several times very successfully. Small chips of brick and warm colored stones might be added to the other aggregates in order to relieve the monotony of the gray walls.

The inside of the house will be plastered. The beams supporting the second floor are to show and be plastered. Fireplace will be treated simply in

tile and concrete. Whatever other decorations are used, they should be quiet and in keeping with the character of the house.

Concrete and cement have been used wherever feasible. Practically, the house is absolutely fire-proof. Although small, there is no waste space.

ESTIMATE.

Excavation	$55.00
Concrete	3,200.00
Lumber	200.00
Mill work	275.00
Plastering	100.00
Painting and glazing	80.00
Hardware	40.00
Tiling	50.00
	$4,000.00

Cubic contents, 23,130 cubic feet.

COMMITTEE'S COMMENTS.

This design, which is most acceptable for the artistic treatment of the conditions which its author has imposed, calls for complete monolithic

construction—walls, floors, and roof, except partitions, which are blocks. The simplicity of the design makes this possible within the sum stated, and the endeavor is quite worthy of recognition. The size of the building is necessarily small because of the high cost of such construction, and we recommend that the concrete roof (which is, moreover, impracticable) be changed to frame and the cost thus reduced. The method specified for treating the exterior wall surfaces, namely, "While the concrete is being placed in the forms, the part next to the forms be pressed back with shovels, thus allowing the smaller stones and concrete to work their way to the front, giving a texture like pebble-dash," will not, we fear, produce that result. For pebble-dash, we recommend a careful selection of the aggregate and a mixture not too wet, about the consistency of jelly. By removing the forms the day after laying and washing the surface to remove the next skin of cement, the particles of the aggregate will be exposed.

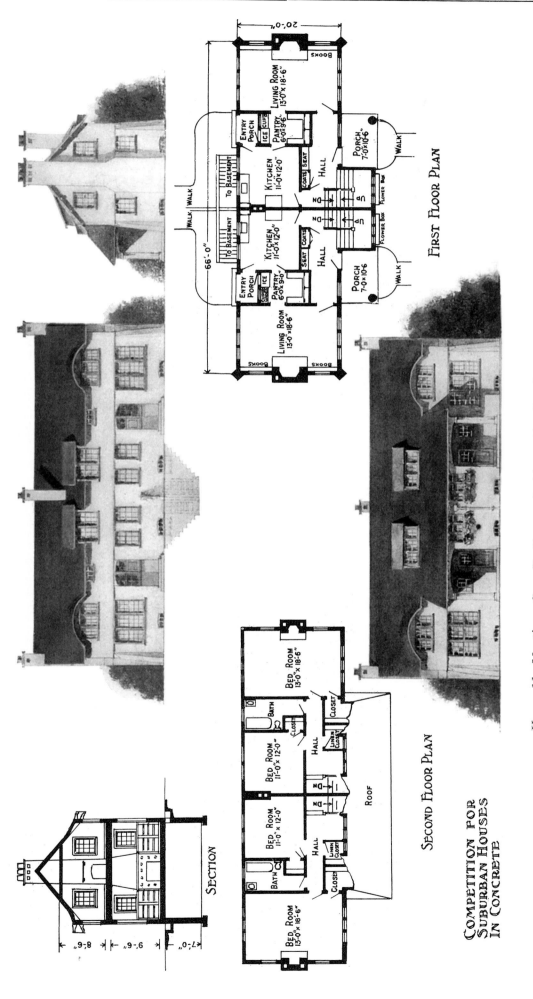

SECTION

FIRST FLOOR PLAN

SECOND FLOOR PLAN

COMPETITION FOR
SUBURBAN HOUSES
IN CONCRETE

Honorable Mention—GEO. B. EICK, Architect, 175 Dearborn Street, Chicago

Outside walls to be of concrete, monolithic construction, with bush-hammered finished surface.

Reinforced lintels over large openings.

Basement walls 12 inches thick.

Above basement 9 inches thick.

Furred and plastered inside.

Outside window sills to be 9x9-inch reddish brown quarry tile, laid to form a drip.

Outside color scheme.

Cement work to be a light brownish tan, made by putting tints in the cement.

Roof stained brown.

Woodwork dark reddish brown.

Inside partitions, first story, hollow concrete blocks, 4 inches thick, plastered directly on concrete blocks.

Lintels over openings to have light reinforcement.

Inside partitions in basement, which are bearing, to be 9-inch hollow concrete blocks; those not bearing, 4-inch hollow block.

Second story inside partitions, 2x4-inch wood studs with lath and plaster.

Wood joists and rafters, every third joist anchored into wall.

Under floor of ⅞-inch boards, ⅞-inch sheathing.

Plates under rafters anchored into wall.

Shingle roof.

Finished floor in living room and hall to be oak, kitchen and pantry to be maple.

Tile floor in bathroom.

Remainder of first and second story floors of yellow pine.

Cement floor in basement and porch.

Finish throughout, except bathroom, to be yellow pine for staining, bathroom white wood for enamel.

Plaster in hall, living room and large bedroom to be sand finish, remainder of plaster hard white finish.

ESTIMATE.	
Excavating	$120.00
Concrete walls and partitions and tile window sills and chimney caps	1,075.00
Carpentry and interior finish	1,580.00
Plastering	285.00
Sheet metal	60.00
Concrete floors in basement and areas	175.00
Glazing	115.00
Brick work for mantels and hearths	55.00
Tile floor in bathroom	60.00
Painting	285.00
Hardware	95.00
Miscellaneous	95.00
	$4,000.00

Cubic contents, 39,486 cubic feet.

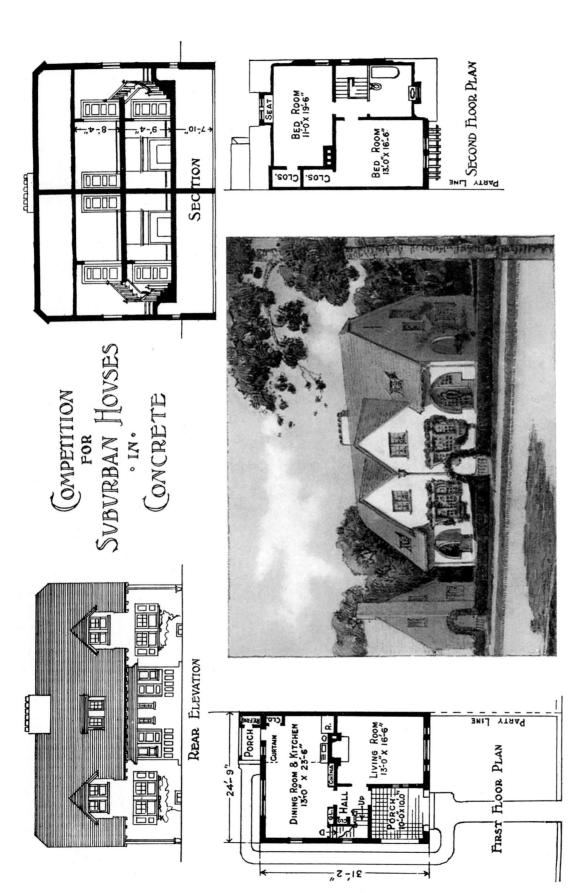

COMPETITION FOR SUBURBAN HOUSES IN CONCRETE

SECTION

SECOND FLOOR PLAN

BED ROOM
11'-0" x 19'-6"

BED ROOM
13'-0" x 16'-6"

CLOS.

CLOS.

SEAT

PARTY LINE

REAR ELEVATION

FIRST FLOOR PLAN

DINING ROOM & KITCHEN
13'-0" x 23'-6"

LIVING ROOM
13'-0" x 16'-6"

PORCH

PORCH
10'-0" x 10'-0"

HALL

REFRIG.

CLO.

CLO.

CHINA

CURTAIN

PARTY LINE

24'-9"

31'-2"

Second Prize—GEORGE S. IDELL, Architect, 1117 Harrison Building, Philadelphia

It is purposed to build the semi-detached houses, accompanied herewith, for the sum of four thousand dollars ($4,000), or the half of that sum for one house.

The outside walls and party wall, from footings to roof, shall be built of 12-inch and 6-inch reinforced monolithic concrete.

The outside walls above the grade shall be furred and plastered, and on the outside face shall be bush-hammered.

Inside partitions, throughout, shall be of 3-inch concrete blocks, on which the plaster shall be directly applied. *   *   *   *   *   *

Plastering.—Two (2) coat work.

Lumber.—2x10-inch hemlock joist, 16-inch O. C., 2x8-inch hemlock, rafters 2 feet O. C.

Millwork of Tennessee poplar.

Oak for first floor; hard rift pine for second. Floors stained and millwork painted white. Porch to be paved with brick, laid flat. Fireplaces to have brick faces and hearths.

ESTIMATE.

Excavations, concrete, walls and partitions.	$1,100.42
Brick pavement	28.00
Stairs	60.53
Lumber, carpenter, roofing and mill work.	2,300.00
Finished fireplaces	180.00
Painting and glazing	50.00
Gas-piping	40.00
Plastering	179.00
Miscellaneous, hardware and lighting fixtures	62.00
	$4,000.00

Cubic contents, 14,388 cubic feet.

COMMITTEE'S COMMENTS.

This is an excellent design in all respects, save only cost, which in monolithic construction would, in spite of the simple outlines, probably exceed the sum stipulated. We feel, however, that the design could be "photographed down" without difficulty to a size which would bring it within the sum. It is, in fact, a more excellent design than the "first prize" (shown on opposite page), and but for this one questionable item would have been placed first.

COMPETITION FOR SUBURBAN HOUSES IN CONCRETE

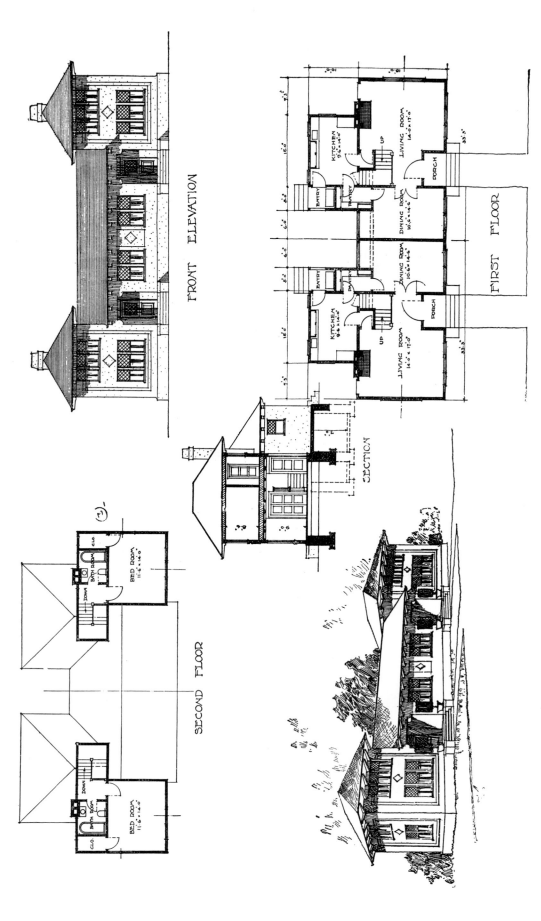

FRONT ELEVATION

SECOND FLOOR

SECTION

FIRST FLOOR

First Prize—ANDREW LINDSAY, Architect, 64 Center Avenue, New Rochelle, N. Y.

The foundation walls up to the level of water table and entrance steps will be of monolithic concrete cast in the usual manner in wood forms. The upper walls will be built of hollow concrete blocks with bush-hammered face. Special blocks to be cast to form paneling and projections.

The roof brackets will be concrete cast in wood mould and soffit of roof projection will be plastered with cement on metal lath.

Chimneys will be built of hollow concrete blocks. Main partitions throughout will be of 4-inch concrete blocks.

Minor partitions will be 2x4-inch spruce lathed. Floor and roof beams will be 2x10-inch spruce.

The inside of exterior walls, concrete partitions and walls and ceilings which have been lathed, will be given two coats of plaster floated to a rough sand finish.

The exterior walls will be a light granite pink in tone and the projecting rafter-ends and roof shingles will be stained silver gray.

The door and window frames and blinds will be painted silver gray.

ESTIMATE.

Excavation	$60.00
Concrete, plastering, etc	2,800.00
Woodwork and millwork	875.00
Electric wiring or gas-piping	50.00
Painting and glazing	90.00
Hardware	85.00
	$3,960.00

Cubic contents, 33,600 cubic feet.

COMMITTEE'S COMMENTS.

Interesting design, with well broken surfaces relieving the monotony which usually results from the use of concrete blocks. Rooms well lighted and airy. The dining-room could be easily transformed into a bedroom and the room squared by cutting the pantry in half. The bush-hammered blocks specified give a good texture, although somewhat expensive.

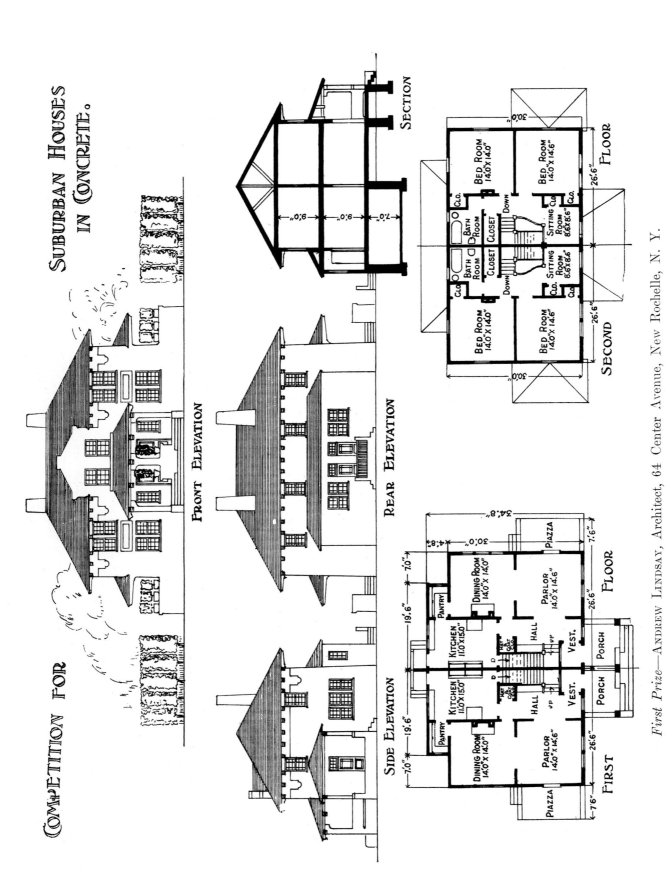

COMPETITION FOR
SUBURBAN HOUSES IN CONCRETE.

FRONT ELEVATION

REAR ELEVATION

SIDE ELEVATION

SECTION

SECOND FLOOR

FIRST FLOOR

First Prize—ANDREW LINDSAY, Architect, 64 Center Avenue, New Rochelle, N. Y.

The foundation walls up to the level of first floor beams, the entrance porches, verandas, balustrades and posts will be of monolithic concrete cast in the usual manner in wood forms. The upper walls will be built of hollow concrete blocks with a bush-hammered face.

The roof brackets will be concrete cast in wood mould and soffit of roof protection will be plastered with cement on metal lath.

Chimneys will be built of hollow concrete blocks. Main partitions throughout will be 4-inch hollow concrete blocks.

Minor partitions will be 2x4-inch spruce lathed. Floor beams will be 2x10-inch spruce. Roof beams 2x10-inch spruce.

All partitions and ceilings and inside of exterior walls will be plastered with two coats floated to a sand finish.

The exterior walls will be light gray in tone; the shingles of roof will be stained silver gray, the door and window frames and blinds will be painted apple green.

ESTIMATE.

Excavation	$70.00
Concrete construction, plastering, etc.	3,950.00
Carpentry, mill work, etc.	1,575.00
Electric wiring	80.00
Painting and glazing	115.00
Hardware	105.00
	$5,895.00

Cubic contents, 61,000 cubic feet.

COMMITTEE'S COMMENTS.

The floor arrangements are commodious, and the exterior pleasing from its simplicity and suggestive of the use of concrete. It is to be regretted that, although the specifications give the foundations to first floor level of concrete and the walls above of bush-hammered blocks, the author has not shown his textures, as it would have added to the interest of the surfaces.

SECTION

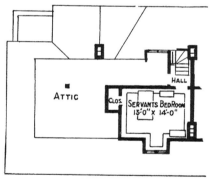

ATTIC PLAN

STORY HEIGHTS - BASEMENT 7'-0", FIRST STORY 9'-0"
SECOND STORY 8-6", ATTIC 8'-0" ALL CLEAR
OUTSIDE DIMENSIONS OF HOUSE 32'-0"x74'-0"
ONE EIGHTH SCALE.

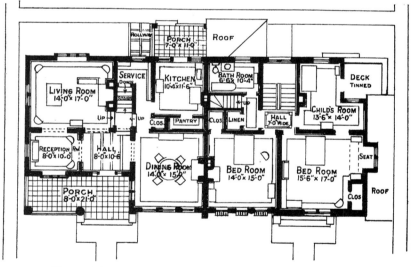

FIRST FLOOR PLAN   SECOND FLOOR PLAN

B³ COMPETITION FOR SUBURBAN HOUSES IN CONCRETE

First Prize—EUGENE WARD, JR., Architect, 11 East Twenty-fourth Street, New York

Outer walls and porch posts to be of monolithic concrete construction. Cellar and porch floors to be of concrete. Outer walls to be 8 inches thick, cemented on the outside and furred with wood furring strips and plastered on wood lath on the inside. Outside walls to have roughcast finish, stained. Chimneys to be lined with flue tile. Cellar under whole house.

All piers in basement, partitions on first floor, and main bearing partitions on upper floors to be of hollow cement blocks, plastered.

Floor joists 2 in. x 10 in., 16-in O. C. Rafters, 2 in. x 6 in.

Minor partitions to be 2-in. x 4-in. studs lathed and plastered.

All floors double with hard pine upper floors. Trim to be cypress stained. Sash of white pine painted. All glass D. S. A. Hardware of good

grade. Fireplaces of selected hard-burned brick. Roof shingled with red asbestos cement shingles. Balcony at second story front bed room to be of 1/16-inch flat steel, riveted and painted black.

ESTIMATE.

Excavation	$160.00
Concrete and cement work	4,050.00
Carpentry	2,000.00
Trim	1,800.00
Painting, etc.	350.00
Hardware	250.00
Tin work	125.00
Wiring, etc.	250.00
	$8,985.00

Cubic contents, 35,000 cubic feet.

COMMITTEE'S COMMENTS.

This design is excellent and individual in both plan and elevation, particularly in elevation. The wall surfaces lend themselves readily to monolithic construction, although plastering on concrete is open to criticism, as already pointed out, where exposed to the weather. The drawings are well drawn and rendered.

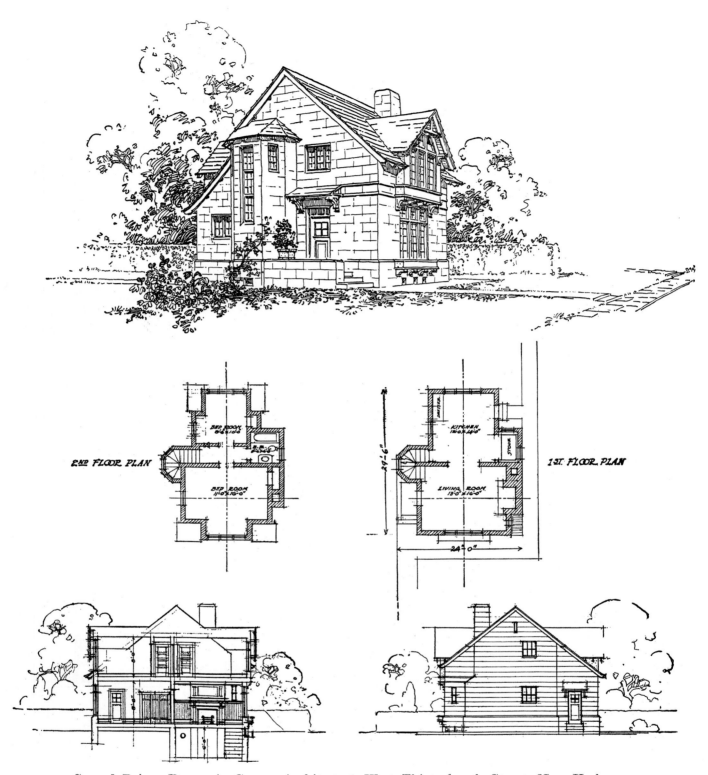

Second Prize—DAVID A. CLOUS, Architect, 1 West Thirty-fourth Street, New York

It is proposed, in the accompanying design, to build all the exterior walls, from footings to roof beams, of concrete blocks, the same to have bush-hammered face wherever exposed above ground. The interior bearing wall, chimney and fireplace shall also be built of concrete blocks, and all lintels occurring in this material to be reinforced with iron ties securely fastened at both ends.

The projecting dormer window, second floor, front elevation, to be stucco on wire lath and stud construction.

All unexposed wood framing of floors and roof to be hemlock. Exterior exposed work to be chest-nut stained. Interior exposed work, white pine, painted.

Roof to be covered with Oregon shingles, laid 4½ inches to the weather.

Height of stories in the clear:

Cellar .... 6' 0"
First floor .... 8' 6"
Second floor .... 8' 0"

ESTIMATE.
(Without plumbing and heating.)

Excavation	$35.00
Mason work	540.00
Lumber, mill work and shingles	500.00
Labor	525.00
Plastering	175.00
Painting and glazing	175.00
Hardware	25.00
Sheet metal	25.00
	$2,000.00

Cubic contents, 10,756 cubic feet (including all projections, porches, etc., from bottom of footings to ridge of roof).

COMMITTEE'S COMMENTS.

Excellent concrete block design. Compact plan, interesting exterior. While the outline of the plan shows a number of angles, these are not prohibitive in inexpensive concrete block construction, as they would be in monolithic construction. The projecting dormer window is of frame, stuccoed on metal lath. Perspective well presented.

COMPETITION FOR SUBURBAN HOUSES IN CONCRETE

SIDE ELEVATION

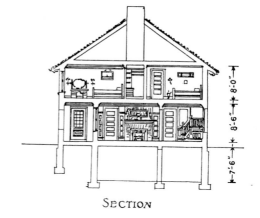

SECTION

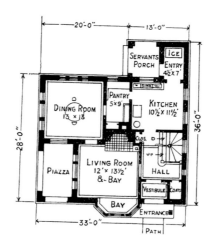

FIRST STORY PLAN

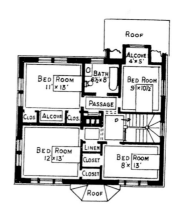

SECOND STORY PLAN

DESIGN A·3·

First Prize—W. CORNELL APPLETON, Architect, Newton Center, Mass.

Monolithic concrete walls. Surface fine picked 4x8x16-inch hollow block partitions in first story.

Chimneys, concrete blocks with skim coat above roof.

Roof, variegated red slate laid in irregular courses.

A monolithic wall with air space could be used for a sum slightly in excess of the above figure.

Cubic contents, 37,052 cubic feet.

ESTIMATE.

Excavating and concrete...................$2,050.00
Lumber 430.00

Mill work............................	350.00
Carpenter work.......................	600.00
Stairs	175.00
Hardware	150.00
Slating	200.00
Plastering	300.00
Painting and staining................	100.00
	$4,355.00

COMMITTEE'S COMMENTS.

This is a remarkably compact plan, with severely simple outlines, well adapted to monolithic wall construction. A single chimney answers all requirements. The relations of the first story rooms to each other are not only practical, but well thought out in dimensions and variety of forms; which is equally true of the second story. The exterior appearance is most pleasing and the drawings well rendered, the perspective sketch in pen-and-ink being unusually clever. The wall surfaces are specified to be finely picked, which gives an entirely satisfactory finish, especially when the aggregates are well chosen.

RESIDENCE OF W. L. STOW, ROSLYN, L. I.   J. R. Pope, Architect
Stucco on Brick

RESIDENCE OF MRS. H. B. JACOBS, NEWPORT, R. I.   J. R. Pope, Architect
Stucco on Brick

RESIDENCE OF MRS. R. GAMBRILL, NEWPORT, R. I.   Carrere & Hastings, Architects
Stucco on Brick

RESIDENCE OF F. M. WHITEHOUSE, MANCHESTER, MASS.   Arthur Huen, Architect
Stucco on Metal Lath

RESIDENCE OF R. M. GILLESPIE, TUXEDO PARK, N. Y.   Howard & Cauldwell, Architects
Stucco on Metal Lath

RESIDENCE OF T. G. CONDON, TUXEDO PARK, N. Y.   E. Wendell, Architect
Stucco on Brick

RESIDENCE OF W. N. WIGHT, WESTWOOD, N. J.   W. N. Wight, Architect
Solid Reinforced Concrete

RESIDENCE AT WESTWOOD, N. J.   W. N. Wight, Architect
Solid Reinforced Concrete

RESIDENCE OF A. W. JOHNSTON, TOLEDO, OHIO   A. W. Johnston, Architect
Stucco on Metal Lath

RESIDENCE OF GEO. O. FORBES, ROCKWOOD, ILL.   Frost & Granger, Architects
Stucco on Metal Lath

WOMAN'S CLUB HOUSE, LOS ANGELES, CAL.   A. B. Benton, Architect

RESIDENCE OF P. DU LONGPIEY, LOS ANGELES, CAL.   Louis Bourgeois, Architect

A FEW TYPES OF CALIFORNIA STUCCO CONCRETE CONSTRUCTION.

RESIDENCE OF DR. FRANCIS KELLOGG, LOS ANGELES, CAL.   Dennis & Farwell, Architects

RESIDENCE OF J. W. SHERLEY, LOS ANGELES, CAL.   Dennis & Farwell, Architects

RESIDENCE OF MRS. E. S. FENYERS, LOS ANGELES, CAL.   Dennis & Farwell, Architects

RESIDENCE OF E. T. BARNUM, PASADENA, CAL.   Kowaski, Architect

RESIDENCE OF GEN. H. G. OTIS, LOS ANGELES, CAL.   J. P. Kremple, Architect

RESIDENCE OF HOWARD VAN D. SHAW, ARCHITECT
LAKE FOREST, ILL
Stucco on Metal Lath

"BLACKWELL," WINDEMERE   Bailie Scott, Architect

COUNTRY HOUSE, RATTON, EASTBOURNE   F. G. Cook, Architect

SOME SAMPLES OF ENGLISH STUCCO CONSTRUCTION

COUNTRY HOUSE, HELENSBURGH   Honeyman, Keppie & Macintosh, Architects

"PARKWOOD," WARGRAVE   Wm. Flockhart, Architect